Shrines of the Saints in England and Wales

Shrines of the Saints in England and Wales

Michael Tavinor

CANTERBURY PRESS

Norwich

First published in 2016 by the Canterbury Press Norwich
Editorial office
3rd Floor, Invicta House,
108–114 Golden Lane,
London EC1Y 0TG, UK

Canterbury Press is an imprint of Hymns Ancient & Modern Ltd
(a registered charity)
13A Hellesdon Park Road, Norwich,
Norfolk NR6 5DR, UK

www.canterburypress.co.uk

British Library Cataloguing in Publication data

A catalogue record for this book is available
from the British Library

978 1 84825 842 6

Typeset by Regent Typesetting
Printed and bound in Great Britain by
CPI Group (UK) Ltd, Croydon

Contents

To the congregation of Hereford Cathedral with gratitude for their enthusiasm and support for *Celebrating the Saints*.

List of illustrations

Acknowledgements

This book grew from an interest in the shrines of the saints through a series of projects developed at Hereford Cathedral during 2005–08, and my thanks are due to my colleagues and to the cathedral congregation for their support. Further interest was generated through academic study at the University of Wales, Lampeter, and my thanks go to Dr Jonathan Wooding, Professor Janet Burton and Dr Robert Pope.

Individual cathedrals have been generous with their support. My especial thanks go to St Albans (Dean Jeffrey John and archivist David Kelsall), St Davids (Fr Harri Williams), Lichfield (Dean Adrian Dorber and photographer Chris Lockwood), Durham (Dean Michael Sadgrove, Lilian Groves, Canon Rosalind Brown and Canon David Hunt), Westminster Abbey (Dean John Hall and librarian Tony Trowles), Canterbury Cathedral (Dean Robert Willis and archivist Cressida Williams), Salisbury Cathedral (Dean June Osborne), Ely Cathedral (Dean Mark Bonney). Dr John Crook has been most generous in sharing with me the fruit of his own researches into medieval shrines. Thanks also to communities of other churches who have supported this project – not least the parish priest at St Thomas RC church, Canterbury, who gave me generous access to the parish archives. Thanks are due to the Hereford team, especially to librarian Rosemary Firman, archivist Rosalind Caird and photographer Gordon Taylor and to Ian Bass, who was a great help in checking various versions. I am grateful, too, to those who helped with questionnaire work at the Hereford shrine, especially Canon Maureen Palmer, Sylvia Green and Joy and Thomas Roderick. The project has been supported by a symposium on shrines of the saints and my thanks are due to Bea Tabor, for her generous help in making this possible.

Final thanks go to Gill Stanley and Julie Anscomb, for their help with the practical aspects of the project.

The shrine of St Thomas of Hereford, icon on canopy gable (2008)

Foreword
by Sir Roy Strong

Although at times statistics would lead us to believe that the Church of England is in terminal decline, every so often something occurs that lights a candle in what all too often seems an engulfing darkness. The renaissance that has occurred in our English cathedrals in the second half of the twentieth century and into the present one is one such light. Within these places the Catholic tradition, inherited from the Oxford Movement and the Caroline divines, has been recast. And it has produced a form of public worship and private piety in tune with aspects of the present age, one that values things like a dignified liturgy that makes full use of the visual and aural arts in the service of God. Within that there is a strong awareness of history, but one that is not averse to new creativity. And all of that is gathered into what is one shared public space open to anyone, one with areas whose association is articulated by the presence of the altar, the pulpit and the font.

These of course epitomize corporate liturgical action involving both priest and people, calling at least for words and generally music and movement. And that leaves a need for a space that calls for none of these things, except an outpouring of the human heart in prayer in a place set apart, one that is silent and mysterious and whose sanctity is made manifest by its association with the remains of a holy person or saint. And, I think, the fact that the saint or holy person is local, 'one of us' as it were, adds an immediacy and a reality. That seems to me one of the driving forces behind the renewal of shrines in our cathedrals, the thought that this or that person was just one of us walking the streets outside just as we do. I have never forgotten being asked to speak from the pulpit on the annual celebration of the Saints of the North in Durham Cathedral – an event that involves the whole community in procession round that majestic building, visiting the shrines of mighty saints like Cuthbert but also calling to our minds those who succoured the poor in the Victorian age.

Michael Tavinor here explains well the tortuous path within the Anglican Church that has led us to where we are now. No one as far as I know has expressed it better than T. S. Eliot in these memorable lines from *Murder in the Cathedral*:

For the blood of thy martyrs and saints
Shall enrich the earth, shall create the holy places.

For Eliot, the martyr's blood represents that of Christ, and the ground it falls on is forever sanctified. Whether trampled over by armies or visitors, from this ground come the springs that 'renew the earth'.

Sir Roy Strong
The Laskett
November 2015

Candles lit at the shrine of St Thomas of Hereford

Preface

The shrines of the saints in churches and cathedrals were at the heart of medieval religion. In a world of darkness and uncertainty, the saints promised encouragement and healing; no wonder their shrines became places of pilgrimage and popularity. Shrines ensured prestige for cathedrals and the certainty of regular income; the proper housing of shrines led to ambitious building campaigns and, perhaps most important of all, enabled people from all sections of society to share in the intercession of the saints.

All of this was swept away at the Reformation and the shrines fared worst of all, representing all that the Reformers detested – wealth, indulgences and a God hedged round by 'lesser beings'. It has always been inferred that little or nothing of the former glory of shrines remained – a very different story to the mercy shown in Luther's Reformation. This book challenges this view and, after a survey of the medieval shrines of England and Wales and their background, presents evidence proposing that, in small and subtle ways, the tradition was never quite lost.

Impetus for a 'renaissance' of the shrines came in the nineteenth century, with the re-emerging Roman Catholic Church and the Oxford Movement. Each tradition had its own focus and differences, but both raised the profile of the saints in their church communities.

At the same time, cathedrals were rediscovering their own mission and, in many and varied ways, seeds were being sown which would lead to a fuller discovery of what the Reformation had lost.

Research, never before published, charts the course of this 'renaissance', and how both Roman and Anglican communions contributed to the development. Of particular relevance is material focusing on three case studies – Westminster, Chester and Hereford – and how their shrines survived in very different circumstances during the post-Reformation period. Important, too, is the extraordinary 'Tooth saga' at Canterbury (1929–31), which showed how far the Anglican Church had to go during the twentieth century in reinstating shrines of the saints with any conviction.

However, the last 60 years have seen huge developments in the cathedral world – in the theology they have increasingly embraced, pilgrimage, commercialism and an inclusive agenda. The final section of the book puts this in context, focusing on theological themes and presenting a survey of 'restored' shrines, together with empirical evidence and some reflections on what this 'renaissance' may mean for pilgrims and visitors today.

The history of medieval shrines has been well documented, through James Charles Wall's *Shrines of British Saints* (1905) and John Crook's magisterial survey *English Medieval Shrines* (2011). However, no attempt has yet been made to analyse the fate of shrines post-Reformation and to chart their influence in the Church of today. It is hoped that this book may help, to some extent, in addressing this area. Inevitably, the study has focused on cathedrals and their shrines – the world I have inhabited and know best – but a nod has been made to important shrines outside this area, notably Walsingham and Pennant Melangell in Wales. Inevitably, I have had to be selective in the number of shrines discussed. My apologies to my fellow deans for any omissions!

Michael Tavinor

I

Shrines of the saints – a vital part of medieval religion

The anonymous author of the *Rites of Durham*, writing in about 1590, gives us stark contrasts between the glories of the cathedral church as it had been in about 1520, with its shrines and monuments, and the same church 40 years later, after the great iconoclastic ravages of the 1540s and early 1560s. As one of the last survivors of the pre-Reformation regime in Durham, the author felt impelled to write down what he remembered of the church in its glory days, not least for the sake of posterity.

Thus he writes of the shrine of St Cuthbert:

> Six silver bells were attached to this rope, so that when the cover was raised the lovely sound of bells drew all people in the Church to the Shrine to offer their prayers to God and holy St Cuthbert, and see the marvellous decorations upon it … Shortly after the Suppression of the abbey they were all taken down, damaged and defaced in order to efface all memory of them, despite the fact that they signified great honour to the Realm and enhanced the glory of the Church.[1]

This extract provides a clue to the many ways in which shrines of the saints in English cathedrals influenced the life and spirituality of these great churches. The writer sees the shrine as a focus for human prayer and devotion – a key part of the apparatus of the cult of saints – and as a repository for the relics of the saint. More darkly, he also sees the shrine as a focus for controversy and destruction. The shrines of the saints were, within the period of 30 years, both the most loved and the most hated part of English church life.

The importance of shrines in the medieval cathedral

At the time of the Norman Conquest only eight cathedrals had major shrines, and these were mostly of early bishops such as Cuthbert of Durham and Chad of Lichfield.

However, by the time of the Reformation 14 of the 19 cathedrals had at least one major saint.

To this we must add shrines in abbeys and churches – St Albans, Bury St Edmunds, Pennant Melangell, Ilam and many more. To those of major, minor and local saints we must also add the great Marian shrines, of which Walsingham was the supreme example. It is not over-stating the case to say that the shrines of the saints were fundamental to medieval religious life and practice.

Shrines – relics, healing and pilgrimage

The saints were at the heart of the practice of religion in the Middle Ages. Imagine attending mass in a village church in the fifteenth century. As you knelt there, and peered through the rood screen to glimpse the elevation of the host, your eyes would have been drawn, inevitably, to the great doom painting above the chancel arch. In this, Christ sits in judgement on all, on the last day – the blessed are conducted to the heavenly realms, while the damned are pitchforked into the jaws of hell. Part of your task as a believer was to avoid the latter fate. For this you needed the intercession of the saints. To the average worshipper, God was a distant and vengeful being and even his Son came across, in the doom painting, as unsympathetic. The saints were the ones who knew the heights and depths of human existence and who could sympathize and, more importantly, pray to God for mercy for those remaining on earth. Town and village churches were full of small shrines – to local saints, to saints who had a particular influence over some forms of sickness, or the weather, and many wills made provision for the establishing or maintenance of a saint's shrine.

Eamon Duffy, in his writings, has shown the true extent of these practices – practices so lodged in the psyche of the medieval mind that they continued, often secretly, after the Reformation had outlawed them.

While nearly every parish church had its saint's shrine, it was the great cathedrals and abbeys of England and Wales that maintained the most consistent devotion to the saints, and their great edifices were often built and developed because of the presence of the remains of a saint within them.[2]

The physical remains of a saint were crucial to this devotion. Indeed, saints' relics inspired the medieval faithful with a sense of power and mystery. It was believed that the bodies of the saints could transmit the healing powers of God and that a miraculous cure could be obtained by simply touching the shrine and by offering prayers to the saint buried there.

Writers like Ben Nilson and Ronald Finucane have made detailed studies of individual cathedrals and have shown the huge numbers who visited shrines during the medieval period.[3]

At the shrine, pilgrims said their prayers and often left votive offerings, in thanksgiving to the saint for a favour granted. At the 1307 visit by commissioners to Hereford, an inventory was made of the non-monetary offerings made at the shrine of St Thomas Cantilupe:

170 ships in silver and 41 in wax
129 images of men or their limbs in silver, 1424 in wax
77 images of animals and birds of diverse species
108 crutches
3 vehicles in wood and 1 in wax, left by cured cripples
97 night gowns
116 gold and silver rings and brooches
38 garments of gold thread and silk.[4]

Votive offerings left for the saint often corresponded to the healing experienced or to the favour granted – the 97 night gowns mentioned in the Hereford offerings refer to gifts left by women who had been granted the gift of a child after prayer at the shrine.

Candles left at the shrine were often of differing length, corresponding to the length of the wick, measured against the height of the sick person, when prayer to the saint was made.

People would travel long distances to visit cathedrals and their shrines. The journey could be seen as a penance but it was also an opportunity to leave behind everyday life and to examine one's life from afar. Most pilgrimages were made to local shrines, and journeys overseas to Santiago de Compostela, Rome or Jerusalem were comparatively rare; but many medieval Christians would have aspired to make at least one major pilgrimage during their lifetime.

Shrines – symbols of prestige

Shrines in cathedrals gave power and prestige. Their presence meant large offerings from pilgrims and cathedral authorities would stop at nothing in obtaining these treasures. Cathedrals without relics felt inadequate; during a visit to Fécamp, Bishop Hugh of Lincoln was driven to biting off a piece of Mary Magdalene's bone to take to his own cathedral, while raiding parties from other cathedrals were a frequent hazard.

Bishops would spend a whole period of office working towards the canonization of a predecessor. Bishop Richard Swinfield of Hereford worked tirelessly to ensure that his predecessor Thomas Cantilupe achieved saintly status, but, even though he presided over commissions and enquiries from 1287 until his death 30 years later, he failed to witness the great occasion. Others were less successful in achieving the prize. William de Marchia was bishop of Bath and Wells from 1293 until 1302; Wells was desperate for him to be canonized as it lacked a great saint, and a shrine was built in anticipation, but, as it turned out, in vain.

Hereford Cathedral also had high hopes for another bishop, Robert Bethune, and the community set up a collecting box for pilgrims' offerings – but the desired canonization never materialized.

Those cathedrals that did possess shrines used them in the generation of income – the fourteenth-century central tower of Hereford Cathedral with its ballflower ornamentation was paid for almost entirely from the offerings of pilgrims. Indeed, the level of pilgrim offerings was a sure indication of the numbers visiting, and quite often levels of giving dropped dramatically when a saint lost popularity or when a shrine was eclipsed by a 'newcomer' in a nearby establishment.

Shrines – a great leveller of society

All classes undertook pilgrimages to shrines, as seen in Chaucer's *Canterbury Tales* – indeed, the shrines 'gave permission' for even the lowliest members of society to make their entry into the cathedral. Sometimes special arrangements were made for the movement of pilgrims around the cathedrals *en route* to the shrine; at Canterbury a corridor passes below the pulpitum, to allow pilgrims entrance while the offices were being chanted in the choir. At Hereford new processional routes were made for pilgrims as they journeyed to the shrine in the Lady Chapel – these routes were lined with the tombs of bishops, proclaiming to all who came that they were on their way to visit the shrine of one of the company of bishops who had 'succeeded', and had achieved sainthood.

While at the shrine itself pilgrims would have said their prayers together; elsewhere distinctions were observed – the richer pilgrims would have stayed within the precinct walls, perhaps with high-ranking clerics, whereas ordinary pilgrims would have been housed in hospitals and inns outside the walls.

Visits to shrines generated a whole industry of 'souvenirs' and keep-sakes, such as phials of water obtained from contact with the relics of St Thomas Becket at Canterbury, or the pilgrim badges worn by all. The quality of this merchandise was often not of the best; that sold at Ely gave rise to the term 'tawdry', after the Saxon version of Ely's patron saint, Audrey (Etheldreda).

Shrines – their architecture

Shrines contributed hugely to the architectural development of cath-edrals in the Middle Ages. Simple at first, Norman shrines could have one of two forms – either a table type as that found at Canterbury, or a *foramina* type. The latter was a stone chest pierced with large holes in the side. The tomb of St Osmund at Salisbury (complete but not *in situ*) and that of St Swithun at Winchester (fragments) are of this type. It is thought that they went out of vogue on account of the number of people who got themselves stuck in the openings, perhaps to be close to the remains of the saint.[5] Later shrines consisted of a stone base supporting an elaborate casket, or *feretrum*, the whole being contained within a chapel behind the high altar – the saint being literally 'lifted high' on his or her canonization. These shrine bases were themselves a noble art form, as described by Nicola Coldstream, who charts their develop-ment and sees in them a reflection of the changing architectural forms of the churches surrounding them.[6] Individual cathedrals have attracted detailed studies of their surviving shrines,[7] while an impressive series of cathedral histories has shown how the presence of a shrine transformed both the interior and exterior of churches and inspired ambitious building programmes.[8] Thus the east end of Canterbury Cathedral was remodelled to house the shrine of St Thomas Becket after the disastrous fire of the 1170s;[9] Winchester's retro-choir was splendidly rebuilt to honour St Swithun;[10] Gloucester's east end was rebuilt by Edward II to honour the tomb/shrine of his father Edward II;[11] and the magnificent east end of Westminster Abbey was Henry III's response to the rehousing of the shrine of Edward the Confessor.[12] Similarly, the central tower of Hereford Cathedral was rebuilt as a result of offerings at the shrine of St Thomas Cantilupe.[13]

The presence of a shrine in a cathedral gave rise to the development of ever more elaborate chantry chapels, which crowded around the shrine, jockeying for positions of honour. Simon Roffey has described how such chantries in Winchester (Bishops Waynflete and Beaufort, near to St Swithun), St Albans (Humphrey, duke of Gloucester near to St Alban) and Canterbury (Henry IV near to St Thomas Becket), impacted on their surroundings.[14]

While many writers focus on examinations of surviving shrines in cathedrals, others use different art forms to assist in showing the appearance of shrines lost at the Reformation. Thus the peerless stained glass in Canterbury Cathedral provides unique evidence for the appearance of the destroyed shrine of St Thomas Becket.[15]

Notes

1 *The Rites of Durham*, J. Raine (ed.), 1842, 'A Description or Briefe Declaration of all the Ancient Monuments, Rites, Customes belonging or beinge within the Monastical Church of Durham before the Suppression', *Surtees Society*, no. 15, Durham: Dean and Chapter; reprinted with additional editorial material by J. T. Fowler, 1900, *Surtees Society*, no. 107; in modern English version edited by R. W. J. Austin, 1985, Durham: Dean and Chapter, p. 5.

2 E. Duffy, 2001/2005, *The Stripping of the Altars: Traditional Religion in England 1400–1580*, New Haven and London: Yale University Press.

3 B. Nilson, 1998, *Cathedral Shrines of Medieval England*, Woodbridge: Boydell Press; R. Finucane, 1977/1995, *Miracles and Pilgrims: Popular Beliefs in Medieval England*, London: Macmillan.

4 B. Nilson, 1999, 'The Medieval Experience at the Shrine', in J. Stopford (ed.), *Pilgrimage Explored*, York: York Medieval Press, p. 105.

5 J. Crook, 1996, 'Recent Archaeology in Winchester Cathedral', in T. Tatton-Brown and J. Munby (eds), *The Archaeology of Cathedrals*, Oxford: Oxford University School of Archaeology, pp. 35–51.

6 N. Coldstream, 1976, 'English Decorated shrine bases', *Journal of the British Archaeological Association*, 129, pp. 15–34.

7 G. Marshall, 1930–32, 'The shrine of St Thomas de Cantilupe in Hereford Cathedral', in *Transactions of the Woolhope Naturalists' Field Club*, vol. XXVII, pp. 34–50.

8 For the best overview, see T. Tatton-Brown, 2010, 'Canterbury and Pilgrimage Shrine Architecture', in C. Morris and P. Roberts, *Pilgrimage – The*

English Experience from Becket to Bunyan, Cambridge: Cambridge University Press, pp. 99–107.

9 P. Collinson, N. Ramsey and M. Sparks (eds), 1995, *A History of Canterbury Cathedral*, Oxford: Oxford University Press, pp. 63–5.

10 F. Bussby, 1979, *Winchester Cathedral 1079–1979*, Winchester: Paul Cave Publications Ltd, pp. 37–49.

11 D. Welander, 1991, *The History, Art and Architecture of Gloucester Cathedral*, Stroud: Alan Sutton, pp. 164ff.

12 E. Carpenter, 1966, *House of Kings*, London: John Baker, pp. 39–42.

13 P. E. Morgan, 1982, 'The effect of the pilgrim cult of St Thomas Cantilupe on Hereford Cathedral', in M. Jancey (ed.), *St Thomas Cantilupe: Essays in his Honour*, Hereford: Friends of Hereford Cathedral, pp. 145–52. See also, on Winchester and St Swithun: P. Draper and A. K. Morris, 1993, 'The Development of the East End of Winchester Cathedral from the 13th to the 16th century', in J. Crook (ed.), *Winchester Cathedral, Nine Hundred Years, 1093–1993*, Chichester: Phillimore, pp. 177–92. On Worcester and St Wulfstan and St Oswald: B. Singleton, 1980, 'The Remodelling of the East End of Worcester Cathedral in the earlier part of the thirteenth century', in *Medieval Art and Architecture at Worcester Cathedral*, Leeds: British Art and Archaeological Association, pp. 105–16. On Ely and St Etheldreda: P. Draper, 1979, 'Bishop Northwold and the Cult of St Etheldreda', in *Medieval Art and Architecture at Ely Cathedral*, Leeds: British Archaeological Association, pp. 8–27. On Lincoln and St Hugh: P. Kidson, 1994, 'Architectural History', in D. Owen (ed.), *A History of Lincoln Cathedral*, Cambridge: Cambridge University Press, pp. 27–46. On Salisbury and St Osmund: T. Tatton-Brown, 1999, 'The Burial Places of St Osmund', *Spire*, 65th Annual Report of the Friends of Salisbury Cathedral, pp. 19–25.

14 S. Roffey, 2008, *Chantry Chapels – and medieval strategies for the afterlife*, Stroud: Tempus; see also A. Kreider, 1979, *English Chantries: The Road to Dissolution*, London: Harvard University Press. H. M. Colvin, 1991, *Architecture and the Afterlife*, London: York University Press. G. Cook, 1947, *Medieval Chantries and Chantry Chapels*, London: Phoenix.

15 M. H. Caviness, 1977, *The Early Stained Glass of Canterbury Cathedral, c.1175–1220*, Princeton, NJ: Medieval Academy of America; 1981, *The Windows of Christ Church Cathedral, Canterbury, Corpus Vitrearum Medii Aevi*, Vol. II, Oxford: British Academy, pls. 118–55 and XIV.

2

The major shrines of England and Wales – a selection

St Alban – England's first martyr

The shrine of St Alban in the late twelfth century, an illustration by Matthew Paris in his Life of St Alban

Alban lived in the Roman city of Verulamium at the beginning of the fourth century. When the Emperor Severus began his persecution of Christians, a priest known as Amphibalus took refuge in Alban's villa. His devotions and holy life aroused the interest of Alban and eventually Alban was baptized by the fleeing priest. When Roman soldiers searched the villa they found Alban, who had received warning, dressed in the priest's robes, while Amphibalus escaped disguised as Alban. Taken before the magistrate, Alban refused to sacrifice to the gods or to disclose the whereabouts of Amphibalus. After a scourging, Alban was led to the top of a hill overlooking Verulamium where he was beheaded, in about 303. The soldier who beheaded him, according to later medieval legend, found that his eyes fell out of his head. The Romans eventually captured Amphibalus and executed him at Redbourn, four miles away.[1] Alban's grave was already the focus of a cult in the early fifth century. It was visited by Bishop (later Saint) Germanus of Auxerre (d. 446), probably in 429.

The Danes burnt the first chapel built over the site of Alban's martyrdom. The Venerable Bede described this church as 'a place where sick people are healed and frequent miracles take place to this day'.[2] Two centuries later, King Offa of Mercia founded a Benedictine monastery on the site, partly, it is thought, as reparation for his own role in the death of Hereford's St Ethelbert in 794. Alban's earthly remains are said to have been rediscovered by King Offa in 793 and placed in a new shrine in the abbey. The Normans rebuilt the abbey church soon after the Conquest, making use of Roman bricks from the deserted ruins of Verulamium.

The shrine underwent many rebuildings. A reconstruction was begun in 1124 by Abbot Geoffrey, but while still under construction it was stripped of its precious metal to provide alms for the poor. Although the reliquary was sufficiently complete to be used in the translation of 1129, it was not finished until the abbacy of Robert of Gorron (1151–66).

The feretory of the shrine appears to have been portable, judging from Matthew Paris' illustration, able to be carried with poles on the shoulders of four monks.[3]

Robert's successor, Abbot Simon (1167–83) is credited with creating, in 1183, an important new table shrine, which included a new outer chest. Matthew Paris describes this work in great detail in his *Life of St Alban*. It was of the 'pillared' type, a rather taller version of the shrine of St Cuthbert. At the same time, Abbot Simon claimed to have discovered at Redbourn the bones of St Amphibalus, and on 24 June 1186 this reliquary was inaugurated and was placed on the south side of the abbey presbytery, to the right of the high altar and next to the shrine of St Alban.

In the early fourteenth century, Abbot John de Maryns (1302–08) resolved to move the saint's shrine base into the enlarged presbytery, while retaining the twelfth-century *feretrum*, which he adorned at great expense – 160 marks. In the end, he built a completely new shrine base – one of the finest achievements of the Dorset marblers, being constructed of Purbeck marble and Totternhoe stone. At the two ends there were magnificent carvings – at one end a figure of King Offa held a model of the church and above it was a 'scourging of St Alban'. At the other end was a scene showing the execution of the saint, with censing angels, so that the celebrant at the shrine altar would have had the scene of Alban's martyrdom 'before his face and in his heart', just like the predecessors who celebrated mass at the high altar with Abbot Simon's *feretrum* behind it.

The lesser shrine of St Amphibalus was moved in the time of Abbot William (1214–35) to the 'middle of the church' where it was surrounded by a grille. The shrine had subsequent moves, including to the north aisle of the presbytery. Finally, in the time of Abbot Thomas de la Mare (1349–96), the *feretrum* was placed on 'a most beautiful new shrine base' created by the Sacrist, Ralph Whitchurch.

The fifteenth-century watching gallery or loft on the north side of the shrine is a remarkable survival. The custodian on duty would look down on the pilgrims from the top gallery, while another would stand by the recessed aumbries and cupboards that held minor relics. Here security would have been particularly important when the protecting cover was raised and the jewelled reliquary exposed for the veneration of pilgrims. The shrine was enriched with many offerings – an antique Roman cameo, so large that a man could not get his hand around it, was taken to women in difficult labour, to whom it brought relief. Henry III gave a rich bracelet, rings and fine cloth; Edward I bequeathed a silver image of himself; and Edward III bestowed some magnificent jewels.

St David – patron of Wales

St David's must have been an important place of pilgrimage and learning from early times and no doubt the display of relics would have been an intrinsic part of that experience. Relics of St David were certainly being venerated at the cathedral in the eleventh century, since in 1081 Gruffudd ap Cynan and Rhys ap Teudur 'went together to the church of St David to pray. There they became faithful friends, after swearing on the relics ...'[4]

The first certain reference to a shrine at the cathedral occurs in 1088, when a reliquary was stolen and stripped of the gold and silver with which it was covered. This may well have been a portable reliquary – capable of being borne in processions and carried into battle.

According to William of Malmesbury, in 962 the relics were seized and found their way to Glastonbury. Bishop Bernard (1115–48) instigated searches for the relics during his episcopate and it appears that they were miraculously rediscovered in 1275 when John de Gamages, prior of Ewenny, was instructed in a dream to dig at a certain place just outside the south door of the cathedral church. The discovery of these relics led to the creation of a *feretrum* which was no doubt complete by 1284 when Edward I and Queen Eleanor came to St Davids on pilgrimage.

The existing shrine, on the north side of the presbytery, dates from this period. It is double-sided. On the presbytery side, the bottom half resembles an altar with a slab or mensa. It is possible the *feretrum* would have been placed on this ledge. The three blind arches above the mensa may have contained images of St David, flanked by St Patrick and another saint (possibly St Denis). Linking the two sides are *foramina*, as seen in the shrines of St Thomas Becket and St Osmund. Certainly the relics of St David were viewed with great importance: a papal decree made it clear that two pilgrimages to St Davids were equal to one to Rome, whence arose the saying, 'Roma semel quantum, dat bis Menevia tantum'.[5]

St Chad – great saint of Mercia

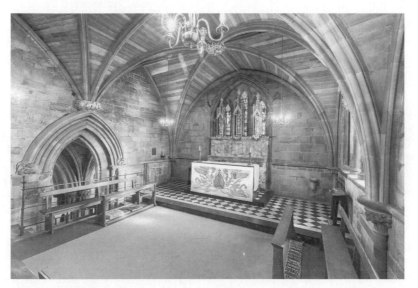

Chapel of St Chad's Head, Lichfield Cathedral

Chad, a Celtic saint who died in 672, spent his life as a missionary in the Saxon kingdom of Mercia. The evidence of many wells named after him suggests that he had huge influence in spreading the gospel in this region. At Lichfield itself, Chad prayed in an oratory beside his well and on winter days is said to have stood naked in the cold water to mortify his flesh.

Chad's remains rested first in a plain wooden shrine in the church-yard of St Mary's at Lichfield. Bede described it as

> a wooden monument, made like a little house covered, having a hole in the wall, through which those that go thither for devotion usually put in their hand and take out some of the dust, which they put into water and give to sick cattle or men to taste, upon which they are presently eased of their infirmity and restored to health.[6]

Bishop Roger Clinton rebuilt the cathedral in honour of the Blessed Virgin Mary and St Chad in 1148 and placed the relics of their new patron saint in a shrine worthy of his memory. There appears to have been a priest of St Chad in Lichfield Cathedral – evidently the custodian of his relics – to whom, in 1241, a special benefaction was made of certain houses in the city for the proper keeping-up of the shrine.

To accommodate the throng of pilgrims and to even more highly exult St Chad, Bishop Walter Langton (1296–1321) completed the rebuilding of the cathedral with the splendid Lady Chapel. Between two piers in this place he installed a new shrine in 1296 at the enormous cost of £2,000 This shrine was moved by Bishop Robert Stretton (1360–86) in 1378 to 'a marble place' in the retro-choir next to the Lady Chapel, with the feretory adorned with gold and precious stones.

In the early sixteenth century, Bishop Geoffrey Blythe enriched the shrine by a gift of two silver images, one of St Chad and the other of St Katherine.

Among other gifts the Sacrist's Roll mentions:

> A morse of pure gold and two gold rings, which were offered that they may be placed in the shrine of St Chad by Dan Thomas de Berekeley and his wife, and one other as catalogued above, replaced in the coffer; and Richard the Sacrist says that they are in the shrine of St Chad; it is well to enquire of John, his predecessor as to the truth of this.[7]

These words suggest that the gifts of jewels were enclosed with the relics and that the coffer was never opened for the purpose simply of counting the riches therein.[8]

At some stage the separated head of the saint, placed in a head reliquary, stood in the Chapel of the Head of St Chad, south of the choir in Lichfield Cathedral. From the Sacrist's Roll it is clear that this painted wooden *chef* lived in an iron-bound coffer enclosed in another chest.

Certainly, in this chapel there is an aumbry, no doubt originally used for the storage of relics, and the head of St Chad and other relics would have been displayed to pilgrims from the chapel's balcony. Indeed, a special shrine-keeper is attested in 1481: the 'custos capitis sancti Cedde'.[9]

Relics of St Chad were preserved in two other locations, one an arm shrine and the other a portable shrine. Whether these were kept in the shrine behind the high altar or with the numerous other relics in the sacristy or in the relic aumbry in the Chapel of St Chad's Head is unknown.

St Etheldreda – indomitable saint of the Fens

In 673 Etheldreda, daughter of Anna, king of East Anglia, established a convent on an island among the Fens and served as its abbess until her death five years later. During her last illness, in 679, Etheldreda endured a tumour in her throat, which she interpreted as punishment for her youthful pleasure in wearing splendid necklaces.

St Etheldreda at Ely Cathedral: the exhumation of her incorrupt body

About 685, Abbess Sexburga, the saint's sister, resolved to translate the bones of Etheldreda from their wooden coffin in the community cemetery to a more suitable shrine. She sent some monks to the deserted Roman camp at Grantchester, where they found a beautifully carved white marble sarcophagus, with which they returned to Ely with much rejoicing. On 17 October 695 the abbess and nuns saw the miraculously incorrupt body transferred to a new tomb set inside the abbey church itself – an event described in detail by the Venerable Bede, and repeated in expanded form in Book I of the twelfth-century compilation of historical texts relating to Ely, known as *Liber Eliensis*. In addition to the discovery of Etheldreda's body as incorrupt, contemporary witnesses suggest that the wound caused by the tumour had been miraculously healed. The site of the original grave remained marked by the appearance of a miraculous spring.

In 870 the devastating Danes invaded Ely. Supposing the marble chest to contain treasure, one of them with repeated blows cracked the stone cover and, according to the *Liber Eliensis*, his eyes immediately emerged from their sockets.[10] No one else dared to touch it and the body of the saint remained undisturbed. When Cnut, the king, visited Ely his queen Emma gave a purple cloth worked with gold and set with jewels to adorn the shrine. Thomas the Chronicler, a monk of Ely, declared that none other could be found in the kingdom of the English of such richness or beauty in workmanship.[11]

With the building of the new choir by Abbot Richard (1100–07) it became necessary to remove the shrine, and, in 1106, on the feast of the former translation, with great pomp the marble shrine was solemnly translated to a position behind the high altar.[12] At the same time the bodies of St Etheldreda's sainted relatives were moved – St Sexburga was placed eastwards of Etheldreda's shrine, St Ermenilda, her niece, on the south side, and St Withburga on the north side. At the service, Bishop Herbert of Norwich preached a sermon on the life and miracles of the saint. At that exact moment, a terrifying storm is said to have broken out. Archbishop Anselm, who had been unable to attend the ceremony, heard the thunder from Canterbury and uttered a dire warning that few of the participants who had viewed the body of St Withburga would survive the year.

The only evidence of the appearance of this shrine – still with its Roman sarcophagus – appears to be on a painted panel dating from the fourteenth or fifteenth century. The panel, found doing duty as a cupboard door in Ely, probably originally served as a retable or altar piece in the conventual church. The last of the four scenes of Etheldreda's life shows the placing of the body in the marble coffin, the sculptures on it being consistent with Roman design of the time of the occupation of Britain.

Around this coffin was built the outer case of the shrine, which contemporary accounts suggest was magnificent:

> The part of the shrine which faces the altar is of silver, adorned with prominent figures, excellently gilt; round the glory are seven beryls and chrystals, two onyxes and two Alemandine stones and twenty-six pearls ... the left side of the shrine is silver, well gilt, adorned with sixteen figures in relief, four score and fourteen large chrystals, and with one hundred and forty-nine small chrystals and transparent stone.[13]

In the thirteenth century, the fine six-bay presbytery was built by Bishop Northwold to house the shrines and to provide more room for pilgrims. On 17 September 1252 the present church was dedicated, and into the presbytery, east of the high altar, St Etheldreda and her three companions were again translated, together with the reputed relics of St Alban, in the presence of King Henry III and his son, Edward.

St Cuthbert – shepherd boy to bishop

Cuthbert, a shepherd boy on the hills outside Edinburgh, had seen a vision of the soul of St Aidan being carried to heaven by the angels. This experience led him to become a monk at Melrose Abbey, and in the disciplined life of a Celtic monastery he became famous for his learning and holiness; so much so that in 685, much against his will, he was made bishop of Lindisfarne, the island where his favourite monastery was situated. After two years of missionary and pastoral work throughout Northumbria, he retired to a solitary life on the

Shrine of St Cuthbert, Durham Cathedral

Great Farne island and died there in 687. He was buried on Lindisfarne. The body was examined in 698 and found to be undecayed. When Danish raiders came in 875, the monks of Lindisfarne took their saint's body and wandered with it in search of safety. For 107 years the body rested in a wooden cathedral at Chester-le-Street, where the remains of the old Roman defences offered some protection from attack. In 995, renewed fear of the Danes set the monks wandering again and after a few months' stay at Ripon they turned northwards and came to Durham. There, on the peninsula formed by a sharp bend in the River Wear, the monks made clearings. By 999 enough of the church was finished for it to be consecrated, and the saint's body was enshrined within it on 4 September. Such a famous possession as the uncorrupted body of St Cuthbert brought pilgrims from all over England.

Cuthbert's body remained enshrined in the Anglo-Saxon cathedral until the early twelfth century, although it was temporarily taken back to Lindisfarne in 1069–70, as a result of the 'harrying of the north' by William the Conqueror.

The reconstruction of Durham Cathedral began during the 1090s, with a new Benedictine community in residence. By 1104 the new building was sufficiently complete for the relics to be translated, and on 24 August Cuthbert's body was again inspected and found to be incorrupt. Abbot Ralph of Sees, a future archbishop of Canterbury, was present at the ceremony and pronounced to the assembled company that 'this body lies here, lifeless indeed, but as sound and entire as on that day on which his blessed soul left it on its way to heaven'.[14]

Within the coffin were found the bones of other saints, among them those of the Venerable Bede and the head of St Oswald, and instruments for saying mass.

The translation of the saint took place on 29 August. The body appears to have been placed in the apex of the new Romanesque apse.

Details of the appearance of the shrine may be gleaned from various contemporary descriptions. Abbot Richard of St Albans (1097–1119) was healed of palsy of the hand while climbing up onto the shrine to assist in the translation – with its pillars, the shrine seems to have been an early example of what became known as a 'medieval high shrine'. In addition, pilgrims were able to crawl beneath the slab of the shrine in order to receive the 'holy radiation'. The eastern apse of the church became dangerous and was rebuilt at the end of the thirteenth century in the form we now have it, including the space containing the shrine, which is constantly called the feretory, a space 37 feet long and 23 feet broad, in the midst of which stood the shrine.[15]

In 1372 John Lord Neville of Raby spent £200 on the substructure of the shrine. The work was enclosed in chests in London and conveyed by sea to Newcastle, from where it was taken to Durham. Neville also gave the altar screen, which forms the west side of the feretory or chapel of the shrine. The description given in the *Rites of Durham* conveys some idea of the magnificence of this latest form of the shrine:

> In the midst of the feretory the sacred shrine was exalted with most curious workmanship of fine and costly green marble, all worked with gold and silver, having four seats, or places convenient beneath the shrine for the pilgrims and infirm sitting on their knees to lean and rest in during their prayers and offering to God and holy S.Cuthbert, for his miraculous relief and succour, which being never wanting, made the shrine to be so richly invested that it was esteemed to be one of the most sumptuous monuments in all England, so great were the offerings and jewels bestowed upon it.[16]

St Werburgh – Chester's holy nun

Werburgh was born the daughter of King Wulfhere of Mercia. She took the veil at an early age and became a renowned abbess, retiring with her mother, Ermenilda, to Ely and to the convent founded there by her great-aunt, Etheldreda. Werburgh established and superintended convents throughout Mercia, notably at Weedon (Northants), Threek-ingham (Lincs) and Hanbury (Staffs). Many miracles are associated with her as a sign of her sanctity; it was rumoured that she could 'hang her veil on a sunbeam'.

Werburgh died on 3 February, possibly in 690 (as held by the Chester tradition) or in 699. In accordance with her wishes, her nuns buried her at Hanbury. Nine years later King Ceolred of Mercia (709–16) elevated her mortal remains, insisting that they should no longer lie 'hidden under a bushel'; this phrase, taken from a well-known parable, became common in all papal bulls announcing canonizations from the thirteenth century. It was expected that Werburgh's body would have decayed but, as Henry Bradshaw, the Elizabethan antiquary wrote in his English version of a life of the saint:

> The corps hole and sounde was funde, verily
> Apperyung to them on slepe as she had ben.[17]

Werburgh's body rested at Hanbury until the Danish threat of 875 forced the nuns to bear her relics into the walled city of Chester for safekeeping.

Hugh Lupus, earl of Chester, founded the Benedictine Abbey of St Werburgh in 1093. Built of red sandstone, it occupied the north-east corner of the medieval city. Here the relics were deposited in a feretory of silver, although nothing is known of the appearance of this shrine.

In 1186, when a great fire swept through the city of Chester, the monks are said to have carried the relics of St Werburgh in procession, pleading for deliverance from the flames.

The monks gradually rebuilt the church, adding a Lady Chapel in the thirteenth century (where the shrine now stands). At the eastern end of the north choir aisle, a late Gothic chapel housed St Werburgh's shrine, beneath beautiful star vaulting.

The appearance of the latest shrine can be deduced from the remains reconstructed today. Judging from its style it appears to have been remodelled in about 1340. It had two tiers of richly carved arcading and a host of statuettes, representing the Mercian royal family.[18]

St Swithun – Winchester's episcopal saint

Swithun was bishop of Winchester from 852 to 863 and was probably a former canon of Old Minster, the Anglo-Saxon cathedral at Winchester, founded by St Birinus in the late seventh century. Tradition has it that he was buried in the common graveyard, where rains might fall on his grave and where passers-by might tread. There his body lay for more than a century. Shortly after his consecration in 963, Ethelwold installed monks from Abingdon in the cathedral and clearly felt that a saint was required for the new establishment. He promoted the cult of Swithun and the translation of his body into the cathedral took place on 15 July 971. A sumptuous reliquary was produced at King Edgar's expense, covered with silver and precious stones, and this appears to have survived until about 1450 when it was melted down.

According to the *Annales Wintonienses*, the monks of Old Minster moved into the new cathedral on 8 April 1093. A few months later, again on 15 July, St Swithun's *feretrum* was installed in the new church. Contemporary evidence suggests that it would have been placed near the high altar – an early thirteenth-century wall painting, now in the cathedral library, seems to confirm this.[19]

Some of Swithun's relics found their way to other establishments.

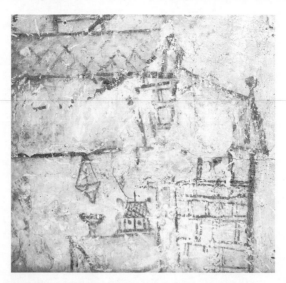

*Reliquary of St Swithun, detail from an early
thirteenth-century wall painting in the cathedral
library, Winchester Cathedral*

During the early eleventh century his head was taken to Canterbury, and by the fourteenth century this had been secured by the canons of Evreux Cathedral. In the early twelfth century one of the saint's arms was taken to Norway, while later in the century his other arm was said to reside at Peterborough. St Albans also claimed a relic of the saint.[20]

Cardinal Beaufort, bishop of Winchester, died in 1447 and in his final instructions he made provision for a reconstruction of the east end of Winchester Cathedral – a scheme that included the construction of a new Great Screen behind the high altar, a new shrine for St Swithun and the building of a chantry chapel for the deceased cardinal alongside the new shrine. As early as 1452 the prior and convent had agreed to create a new silver-gilt 'fontal', which was to be the centrepiece of the new Great Screen. This silver was obtained by melting down the Anglo-Saxon reliquary, and the new reliquary was to be paid for out of Beaufort's estate. The inauguration of the new shrine took place on 14 July 1476 and is described in great detail in a memorandum preserved in the archiepiscopal register of Cardinal John Morton. As well as literary evidence, there is physical evidence for the position of the shrine – the central boss of the retro-choir vault is pierced with a hole, and above the vault are the remains of an iron pulley, attached to a beam, indicating the way the wooden cover over the *feretrum* was raised by means of a counterbalance.

Thanks to the survival of a large number of stone fragments, in Caen stone and Purbeck marble, the appearance of this shrine may be deduced – an elaborate 'high shrine' of the late medieval variety, with 'prayer niches' along each side.

St Edmund the Martyr – royal saint of East Anglia

Shrine of St Edmund, from Lydgate's Life of St Edmund

In 869 Scandinavian invaders captured Edmund, king of East Anglia. Rather than accept freedom in exchange for denying Christ, the young Saxon chose a martyr's death. On 20 November, the Danes tied him to a tree and threw their spears at him (later sources suggest arrows) 'as if in sport'. When he still remained faithful they cut off his head and hid it in a thicket. When a search was made, so Edmund's early biographer states, a voice calling, 'Here! Here! Here!' led them to the thicket, where they found a wolf guarding the head against other wild animals. The head was carried away to Hoxne for burial, the wolf following meekly behind.

In 903 monks removed the body, now miraculously whole again, to a wooden church at Beodricsworth, now Bury St Edmunds. During a further Danish invasion the relics were removed for safety to London, and on their return journey rested in the church at Greenstead-juxta-Onga. On 18 October 1032, Edmund's shrine was dedicated in the presence of King Cnut, who offered the saint a votive gold crown from his own brow. After the Conquest the Normans rebuilt the abbey church, and, on 29 April 1095, Edmund's relics were installed in the presbytery behind the high altar. Many flocked to this shrine – a symbol of the devotion of a young king who had lost his life in the defence of England and the Christian faith. Perhaps the most famous pilgrims were royal visitors – Richard I, who gave land to maintain a perpetual light at the shrine, and Queen Eleanor, who gave many valuable jewels to the shrine.[21]

In 1198 the shrine endured a disastrous fire, although the feretory itself remained unharmed. Abbot Samson set about restoring it, amid many reported miracles. The final translation took place on 18 February 1269 in the presence of Henry III.

Still pilgrims flocked. When Edward I went with his family and court to attend the feast of St Edmund at Bury in 1285, he caused an inspection to be made of all the weights and measures in the town; the profits accruing from that and future inspections he granted for the repair and decoration of St Edmund's shrine.

Among the many miracles recorded is one that suggests that offerings of coins to this shrine were laid in the niches around the base. It is said that a woman who often visited the shrine, under the mask of devotion, when she was bowed in apparent veneration to kiss the shrine, licked up the money and carried it away in her mouth, with dire consequences following. King Henry VI made his pilgrimage to the shrine in 1433, the monks presenting him with a copy of a beautifully illustrated *Life of St Edmund* by one of their number, John Lydgate. It is thanks to Lydgate that we have the best evidence of the appearance of any medieval shrine.

A letter of the Commissioners at the dissolution of the monastery gives some indication of the wealth and magnificence of the shrine. John Williams, Richard Pollard, Philip Paris and John Smyth wrote thus to Thomas Cromwell:

Pleaseth it your lordship to be advertised that we have been at Saint Edmunds-Bury where we found a rich shrine which was very cumberous to deface. We have taken in the said monastery in gold and silver MMMM marks and above, over and beyond as well a rich cross with emeralds as also divers and sundry stones of great value.[22]

The total spoils of plate taken from the abbey in 1538–39 amounted to 2,553 ounces of gold and 10,433 ounces of silver.

St Oswald and St Wulfstan of Worcester – 'supporters' of King John

Oswald, bishop of Worcester, appears to have been recognized as a saint immediately after his death in 992. In the *Life* of the saint, compiled within five years of his death, it was stated that at his funeral some women mourners witnessed a dove and miraculous light – taken to be signs of Oswald's sanctity. He was buried in an elaborate tomb in the cathedral, over which a monument of 'marvellous workmanship' was erected and at the same time some of his relics were translated to York, where he had also been archbishop. The Worcester tomb was situated on the south side of the high altar. On 15 April 1002, Oswald's body was elevated by Archbishop Ealdwulf and placed in a *feretrum*, possibly behind the high altar, in order to give the saint more dignity and to protect his tomb from 'the irreverent'.

Bishop Wulfstan was one of the few Anglo-Saxon bishops allowed to retain his bishopric after the Norman Conquest and he was responsible for the building of the new cathedral. Wulfstan translated Oswald's remains into the new cathedral in 1088–89. According to William of

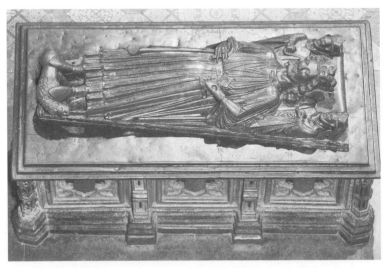

Tomb of King John, with St Oswald and St Wulfstan on either side of the king's head, Worcester Cathedral

Malmesbury, Wulfstan placed the relics, together with those of many other saints, in a reliquary that was an enlarged version of the one Oswald himself had originally created to house relics of St Wilfrid.

Wulfstan, too, was canonized. The beginnings of his cult are to be found soon after his death in January 1095, at the age of nearly 90. People were accustomed to kneel in prayer at the bishop's tomb, and this appears to have hastened the cause for canonization. William of Malmesbury suggests that the tomb was free-standing, with tapering pillars either side of it, an arch over it and the monument protected by a grille, and it was most likely situated on the north side of the choir.

Wulfstan was canonized in 1202 and his cult continued alongside that of Oswald – both had their heads separately enshrined. Pilgrims came in great numbers and 'St Wulfstan's water' became a popular devotional aid. St Wulfstan was translated to a new shrine in 1218, and to this occasion the bishop invited William de Trumpington, abbot of St Albans. On William's return to his own abbey, he triumphantly bore a rib of St Wulfstan. There the abbot erected an altar to the saint, above which he placed the rib, enclosed in gold work of great beauty.

King John held St Wulfstan in great veneration and more than once he made offerings at the shrine – indeed, the intercessions of Oswald and Wulfstan were considered so powerful that King John asked for his own tomb to be placed between the shrines of the two saints, which then stood one at either side of the presbytery.[23]

St Edward the Confessor – patron of England

From the Bayeux Tapestry we gain an impression of the chest in which Edward the Confessor's body was enclosed after his death in 1065 – a rectangular chest, with a gabled roof. The tapestry shows the body on its way to burial in the newly finished church that Edward had built. At the coronation of William the Conqueror in 1066 the new king offered two palls or precious hangings for the monument, and shortly after this erected a sumptuous monument over the tomb, with ornamentation of gold and precious stones.

The tomb was opened in 1101/02 by Abbot Gilbert Crispin and the relics were found to be intact. This encouraged veneration of the king, even though he had not, as yet, been canonized at Rome.

Through the encouragement of Thomas Becket, Edward was declared a saint by Pope Alexander II in 1161. Two years later Henry II had a magnificent shrine made, into which Edward was translated on 13

Shrine of Edward the Confessor, Westminster Abbey, MS University Library, Cambridge

October 1163 – an event described in great detail by the Westminster monk, Richard of Cirencester (fl. 1355–1400). The wooden chest was borne into the church at the head of a great procession, followed by King Henry II, Archbishop Thomas Becket and a great gathering of bishops and nobility.

We have evidence of the appearance of Edward's various shrines from manuscripts in Cambridge University library,[24] dating from about the 1240s – although it is unclear whether the illustrations in the manuscript refer to the original tomb, to the 1163 shrine, or are some kind of prediction of the shrine they imagined the abbey was soon to acquire. One illustration shows the king and archbishop lifting the body from the old to the new tomb, assisted by the abbot and other prelates. Another illustration shows pilgrims venerating the relics, while one of them creeps through an aperture in the base – clearly hoping thereby to receive some relief from infirmity. At the two ends of the shrine, on slender shafts, stand the figures of St John the Evangelist and St Edward – the latter recalling the legend of Edward's generous presentation of his ring to a beggar.

The cult of Edward the Confessor, however, owes its existence mainly to Henry III. The new king had a great devotion to the Confessor and saw Edward as his patron. He resolved to remodel the abbey church as a setting worthy of the burial of his own saintly inspiration, and the new shrine, within the chapel of St Edward immediately behind the high altar, was intended as the focus of the abbey church. It was next to this monument that Henry III elected to be buried, thus initiating the shrine area as a royal mausoleum for the monarchs of England. The shrine was constructed with the finest of materials and decorated with cosmati work. Some of this may have been the work of Abbot Ware, who returned to England from Rome in 1260 bringing with him rich porphyry stone and two workmen – Peter and Oderic – who were skilled in mosaic work to beautify the shrine, on which the name of one 'Roman citizen' can still be read. Many of the jewels ornamenting the shrine appear to have been financed by Henry III himself; one list of expenditure for this suggests the staggering outlay of £1,234 11s.

On 13 October 1269 – the feast of the first translation – the body of St Edward was again translated, this time to its final resting place. The ceremony was one of great splendour, the golden feretory being borne by the aged king, his brother Richard, and Edward and Edmund, his two sons.

By the fourteenth century Edward's fortunes as a saint were waning, however, and he was superseded as patron saint of England by the soldier-saint George.[25]

St Osmund of Salisbury – champion of liturgy

Osmund was promoted to bishop of the new diocese of Sarum in 1078. His chief fame resides in his reputation as a liturgiologist and compiler of the *Consuetudinarium*, known as the Use of Sarum, by which he influenced the Church's services throughout the land. He was a person of great sanctity and was responsible for developing the cult of St Aldhelm, at a time when his fellow Norman bishops were treating Anglo-Saxon saints with disdain. It was Osmund who supervised the translation of Aldhelm's bones in Malmesbury Abbey and who also obtained relics of the saint for his own new cathedral at Sarum.

Osmund died in 1099 and was buried in his cathedral church at Old Sarum, possibly in the eastern choir – miracles were attested at this tomb by the 1170s. At the removal of the cathedral to its present site in Salisbury in 1226, Osmund's body and the bones of other prelates were translated to the new church. His relics were laid in the Lady Chapel and he was invoked as a saint for more than 200 years before he was formally canonized in 1456. It is possible that the tomb-shrine, now placed in the cathedral on the south side of the Lady Chapel, was the

Foramina *tomb-shrine of St Osmund, now relocated in its original position on the south side of the Trinity Chapel, Salisbury Cathedral*

structure brought from Old Sarum and re-erected in the new building. Its form is that of a *foramina* tomb-shrine, with apertures or portholes in each side.[26]

In the process of canonization many miracles were recorded at the tomb – two examples of those mentioning the *foramina* must suffice. John Beaminster, out of his mind, was brought by his friends to the tomb at the start of the Lady Mass, and remained with his head and hands inside the tomb 'until the Agnus Dei was sung'. Likewise a certain 'Loony Tom' ('Thomas furiosus') was brought to the tomb; friends put his hands in the apertures of the tomb and his bonds miraculously fell off.

The canonization was so frequently delayed at Rome and the people flocked in such numbers to the tomb that the canons of the cathedral exhumed the body, placed it in a shrine and venerated him as a saint without waiting for papal authority.

In 1456, thanks to the final efforts of Bishop Beauchamp, the process was concluded and Osmund was declared a saint in a letter from the pope to Henry VI. The chapter at once began to erect a shrine, but it appears not to have been completed until the 1490s. In 1471, a goldsmith from London, Edward Bowden, provided new designs for a silver shrine and in 1485 there was further embellishment. However, despite detailed records of the financial arrangements for the work, surviving documentation provides very little idea of what the monument looked like.

St William of York – saintly archbishop

William Fitzherbert was archbishop of York from 1141 to 1147 and again in 1154 for a few months until his sudden death, perhaps by poison. He was buried in a reused Roman sarcophagus in the nave of the Minster. A few years later, a fire broke out in the city and this spread to the Minster. During the fire a beam collapsed on the coffin lid, breaking it, but miraculously the body of the archbishop appeared undamaged. This perceived miracle led, in part, to the

The fifteenth-century 'St William Window', showing a man presenting an ex-voto in the form of a wax model of his leg, York Minster

development of a cult surrounding Fitzherbert, although official canonization had to wait until 1226, when Pope Honorius III declared his sainthood, after a campaign promoted by Fitzherbert's successor as archbishop, Roger Pont l'Évêque. The canonization may well have been hastened as a response to the 1220 elevation of St Thomas of Canterbury – the second primatial see understandably wishing to enjoy similar prestige. In addition, further miracles were recorded in the late 1290s, including the miraculous oozing from the tomb of oil with saintly powers – a phenomenon recorded by Matthew Paris in around 1223.

In the event, the body was not raised to an elevated position, possibly as the Minster was about to embark on a major building campaign, and so the translation did not take place until 8 January 1284, when William Wickwaine was archbishop. The ceremony for this was lavish – it was attended by Edward I and Queen Eleanor. Indeed, the king had good reason for his devotion to the saint; during the planning of the event, he miraculously survived a fall from a high place – a deliverance he attributed to the saint's intervention.

The new shrine was widely visited by pilgrims, including Margery Kempe, who came to York in 1413 and 1417, but its form is unknown. A few years later, in 1421–23, the famous 'St William Window' was created. This shows the shrine, but its architectural character is contemporary with the window and the artist may well not have intended a realistic depiction.

What we see in the window is a shrine with two storeys, prayer niches and a gabled top. At the west end of the shrine is an altar, and also taps from which pilgrims could draw the holy oil that continued to be a major feature of the cult.

William's head was removed in 1286 and separately enshrined, in a structure richly adorned with jewels and precious stones.

During the 1330s, Archbishop William Melton (1317–40) donated £20 towards the 'new building' of St William's tomb. This was built over the original, empty tomb and appears to have consisted of an arcaded substructure supporting a flat slab, above which was a canopy-like second storey with 12 supporting statues of saints within tall niches. This superstructure was entirely ornamental, given that the body was enshrined elsewhere in the Minster.

In about 1470 the long process of rebuilding the east arm of the Minster in Perpendicular style was coming to a conclusion, after well over a hundred years, and in 1472 the cathedral was reconsecrated to mark the completion of the works. As part of the remodelling, the shrine of St William was reconstructed. Evidence for the work is found in records of donations – in 1471, the rector of Lythe, near Whitby, left ten shillings in his will 'to the construction of the marble base for the feretrum of St William',[27] while payment is recorded for a 28-day journey for Robert Spillesby, Clerk of Works 1466–73, in order to consult specialist marblers, required for the construction of the shrine. The new shrine appears to have been raised on one step, with niches for prayer. It was certainly sumptuously appointed, and the York Inventory of c.1500 mentions the large number of adornments in gold, silver and precious jewels.[28]

Thomas Becket – focus of pilgrimage for Britain and Europe

Thomas Becket was fast-tracked to canonization as a saint. Scarcely had his body been buried in the crypt of Canterbury Cathedral than some of the monks immediately embarked on a mission to Rome to convey their version of the story to the pope. Within a year Alexander III sent legates to investigate the miracles associated with Becket – they carried back with them such relics as the blood-stained tunic and a fragment of the flagstone showing bloodstains. In 1173 the pope officially canonized Becket, making 29 December the Feast of St Thomas of Canterbury.

Foramina *tomb of St Thomas, detail from a window in the Trinity Chapel, Canterbury Cathedral*

Becket was soon revered far beyond Canterbury – from Iceland, where a saga about the saint was composed, to Spain and Sicily, where the saint appears in mosaics of the mid-1170s in the cathedral at Monreale.

In Canterbury itself the monks had buried their prelate beneath the pavement of the axial chapel on the east side of St Anselm's crypt, and shortly after the canonization a tomb-shrine had been constructed over the grave. This monument is shown many times in the early thirteenth-century glass in the ambulatory of the Trinity Chapel at Canterbury and from these depictions we can deduce that it was of the *foramina* type, with apertures to enable pilgrims to access the relics themselves.[29]

Canterbury rapidly became a great pilgrimage centre, rivalling Rome and Santiago de Compostela, and the city of Canterbury became the destination of pilgrimages from throughout England and beyond. The great pilgrim routes from London and Winchester are punctuated with pilgrim chapels, churches and hostels – all part of the huge cult that Becket attracted, and pilgrims returned from Canterbury with pilgrim badges of the saint and with flasks or ampullae filled with water tinged with the martyr's blood.

In many ways the fire of 1174 was almost a happy accident, as it necessitated the reconstruction of the entire east end of the cathedral, thus creating a spectacular setting for a proposed new shrine. The

Chapel of the Holy Trinity was made of ample dimensions for the new shrine; eastwards of that was built a circular chapel, known as 'the Crown of St Thomas' or 'Becket's Crown', which eventually housed an additional shrine with a relic of a piece of bone sliced from the martyr's head.

Becket's remains were translated to their new shrine by Archbishop Stephen Langton on 7 July 1220, in the presence of King Henry III, and subsequently the feast of the 'translation' was celebrated with great solemnity. Magnificent 'jubilees' were held to mark centenary years in 1320 and 1420 – in the latter jubilee year, 100,000 pilgrims are said to have visited the shrine.

We know that the 1220 shrine was the work of Walter of Colchester (d. 1248), who attended the translation, and of Elias of Dereham. Walter was one of an important family of craftsmen who had become monks at St Albans in the early thirteenth century. However, there is little contemporary documentary evidence for the appearance of the new shrine. A scene in the thirteenth-century glass in the Trinity Chapel shows the saint emerging from a *theca* or *feretrum* supported on pillars, rather than from the holes of the *foramina*, and there is a fragment of glass in the church of St Mary, Nettlestead, which gives a glimpse of the new shrine.[30] Certainly it was magnificent. In the early sixteenth century, a Venetian visitor wrote:

> Notwithstanding its great size, it is entirely covered with plates of pure gold. But the gold is scarcely visible beneath a profusion of gems, including sapphires, diamonds, rubies and emeralds. Everywhere that the eye turns something even more beautiful appears. The beauty of the materials is enhanced by the astonishing skill of human hands. Exquisite designs have been carved all over it and immense gems worked delicately into the patterns.[31]

The only other representation of the shrine is more suspect – a drawing preserved in a fire-damaged manuscript in the Cotton collection of the seventeenth century. The very absence of the word 'saint' in its label – 'the forme of the shrine of Tho Becket of Canterburye' – implies a post-Reformation date. The drawing shows a large stone base with the reliquary surmounting it and, most curious of all, a small sketch at the bottom of the page, depicting an open chest with Becket's bones. This depiction appears to have been based on verbal description, probably that of John Stow, whose Annals of *c.*1538 provided the text accompanying the drawing.[32]

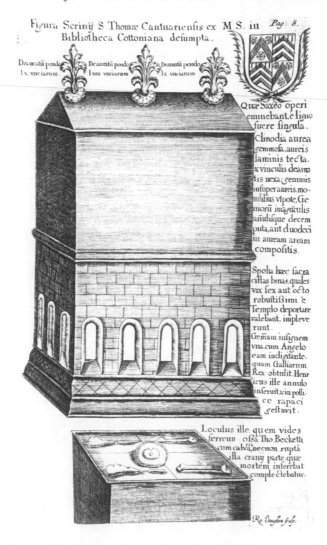

Shrine of St Thomas of Canterbury, drawing purporting to show the shrine, from BL Cotton MS, Tiberius E.viii, fo. 278v, p. 234.

Later artists have attempted to depict the magnificence of the shrine, their paintings often encapsulating the drama and awe and noise surrounding a shrine like Becket's. One representation shows the wooden box-like structure or case, suspended by a rope to a pulley in the roof by which it was raised up or lowered – possibly silver bells attached to the canopy (such as we know were part of Cuthbert's shrine at Durham) alerted pilgrims to an exposition of the relics at regular intervals during the day.

It is probable that the cult of St Thomas was declining in popularity even before Chaucer wrote *The Canterbury Tales* at the end of the fourteenth century, yet on great occasions, such as the Black Prince's funeral in 1376, numbers revived. The only real criticism of the shrine came from a few isolated Lollard heretics, one of whom was executed as late as 1532 for insulting the martyr.

The destruction of the shrine came quickly when the government turned against the 'papist' archbishop who had resisted royal domination in an earlier age. The shrine was destroyed in 1538 and huge cart-loads of jewels and treasures were taken from it. All traces of the shrine were removed and references to Becket were ruthlessly expunged from missals and service books, as Becket was proclaimed a rebel and traitor by royal decree. Parts of the original floor of the Trinity Chapel remain, including a sizeable area of Opus Alexandrium pavement on the west side of the site of the shrine.

St Hugh of Lincoln – saintly bishop

Hugh was born in Burgundy in 1140 and became a monk at Grand Chartreuse.[33] In 1175 he was invited by the English king, Henry II, to become prior of his Charterhouse foundation at Witham in Somerset, which was greatly in need of reform even though it had only recently been founded. In 1186 Hugh was persuaded to accept the see of Lincoln, then the largest diocese in the land. He brought huge energy to the diocese and, together with discerning appointments to key posts, he revived the Lincoln schools and repaired and enlarged the cathedral. Visiting the diocese extensively, he drew together the clergy to meet in synod and generally brought efficiency and stability to the Church. Hugh also showed great compassion for the poor and the oppressed, ensuring that sufferers of leprosy were cared for and that Jews were not persecuted. He died in London on 17 November 1200.

The original burial place of Hugh, in 'an outstandingly honorific tomb', is uncertain, though it has been suggested that it was in a transept chapel of Lincoln Cathedral, demolished in the eighteenth century. Wherever it was, the tomb soon became the scene of miraculous happenings and there was a groundswell of support for his canonization. At this time bishop-saints were undergoing a vogue of popularity, especially those who, like Hugh, upheld the values of Gregorian reform. In 1220 Honorius III canonized Hugh as a 'white martyr' – in other words, one who through this life demonstrated an exceptional witness to Christ. Significantly, the pope added the statement that his body 'should be translated from the place it now is and more honourably situated'.[34]

By 1255, the growing volume of pilgrims convinced the Dean and Chapter to demolish St Hugh's recently completed east end and create an 'Angel Choir' to provide a more sumptuous space for the shrine and for pilgrims. The new choir is one of the most remarkable achievements of the Early English style.[35] Edward I and Queen Eleanor came to Lincoln on 6 October 1280

Feretory of St Hugh of Lincoln in procession, from a window in Lincoln Cathedral

to witness the translation of Hugh's body to its new feretory. When St Hugh was raised from his original resting place, his corpse was found to be in a remarkable state of preservation, a sure sign of sanctity.[36] However, during the upheaval of the translation the head dropped off; far from being regarded as a disaster, however, this was hailed as an example of divine providence, because when the body reached its new resting place it was discovered that the tomb had been made too small to accommodate the saint with his head still attached.[37]

The location of this tomb has long been a matter of speculation, but it was probably situated to the east of the choir screen, making it a focus for the Angel Choir. In common with many such monuments, it had a wooden canopy that could be raised on special occasions, and was surrounded by railings.[38] St Hugh's detached head was relocated in a shrine of its own close by, the surviving remains of which date from 1331. This 'head shrine' took the form of a decorative pedestal on which a portable reliquary stood when it was not being carried in procession.[39] The financial management of the shrine is well documented,[40] and pilgrims appear to have been mainly local and regional. Inventories made in 1520 and 1536 indicate that the shrine was still laden with treasures, 'sapphires, gold images and crosses as well as pearls', despite the dwindling number of pilgrims.[41]

St Richard of Chichester – bishop for the people

The development of the cult of St Richard de Wych, bishop of Chichester (1244–53), is very well documented. He died on 3 April 1253 and in his will directed that his body was to be buried in Chichester Cathedral. According to his biographer, John Capgrave, Richard's sanctity was popularly recognized even before his burial – as his body was being carried to the church, people were touching the bier or the hem of his vestments. Following representation to Pope Urban IV, Richard was proclaimed a saint on St Vincent's day (22 January) 1262. The proclamation did not include the usual instruction that the saint's body should be disinterred and elevated, and so the references to indulgences stated that these would be obtained at the 'sepulchrum' or 'tomb'.

On 16 June 1276 Archbishop Robert Kilwardby, in the presence of the king and many bishops and nobles, translated the body into a silver reliquary. The saint's head was removed during the translation and placed in a silver *chef* in the chapel of St Mary Magdalen. The main reliquary was placed on a platform, protected by an iron grille, fragments of which are thought to survive. Edward I had a particular devotion to the saint, and on 31 March 1296 he and his queen offered gold clasps at the shrine.[42]

In 1478, on the feast of St Richard, such was the crush of pilgrims visiting the shrine that Bishop Storey made new rules regarding the conduct of pilgrims, insisting that instead of carrying staves pilgrims should walk with crosses and banners and in decent order from the west door.

St Thomas of Hereford – aristocratic bishop of the Marches

Thomas Cantilupe (1218–82) was born of a noble family, studied in Oxford and Paris and achieved high office in the state. He became bishop of Hereford in 1275 and was known as a zealous and loving pastor. But he took issue with the archbishop of Canterbury, John Pecham, over questions of episcopal jurisdiction and was excommunicated in 1282. To appeal against this, Cantilupe travelled with his entourage to the papal court, then resident at Orvieto. Although Martin IV received him graciously and an absolution was given, Cantilupe contracted a fever and died at Montefiascone, outside Orvieto, on 25 August 1282. According to the custom of the day, his body was boiled, following which his bones were brought back to Hereford, his heart being deposited in the college

*Shrine of St Thomas of Hereford in the fifteenth-century
(artist's impression), Hereford Cathedral*

of Bonshommes at Ashridge in Buckinghamshire. Cantilupe's bones
were first buried in the Lady Chapel at Hereford Cathedral, and almost
immediately reports of healing at the site of his tomb were circulated.
Such healings became more common from 1287, when his body was
transferred to a tomb in the north transept.[43] Driven by his successor
as bishop, Richard Swinfield (1282–1317), the case for canonization
gained pace and in 1307 a Commission was set up to make enquiry of
the claims. In one of the most detailed of canonization enquiries, over
400 miracles of healing were noted.[44] Cantilupe's healing powers were
said to be so great that on two occasions Edward II made offerings for
his sick falcons to be healed and sent a waxen image of the ailing birds.

By 1320, when the exiled Avignon pope, John XXII, announced
Cantilupe's sanctity and established 2 October as his feast day, Swinfield, the saint's great champion, had died. But work began immediately
on a new shrine to be placed in the Lady Chapel. In December 1320 a
London goldsmith called John of Werlyngworth was making various
ornaments for the shrine, with Purbeck marble supplied by Adam of

Corfe. The translation did not take place until 25 October 1349, when the ceremony was attended by Edward III and Queen Philippa. In this year of the Black Death there was a great hope that such a translation, with honour paid to the saint, would lessen the ravages of the pestilence. Even before 1349, the number of pilgrims was diminishing and the shrine was no longer the draw that it had been in its heyday in the late thirteenth century. But, at its peak, the number of pilgrims made this one of the most frequented shrines in the West Country. Offerings from pilgrims enabled the building of the central tower, with its elaborate ballflower decoration.

Although the Lady Chapel shrine was destroyed, that in the north transept survived.[45] The monument is in two stages. The base, standing on a modern plinth, is decorated with an arcade, each arch containing an image of a seated knight. The substructure supports a Purbeck marble slab, formerly with a brass of the saint and two attendant figures of which only one, portraying Hereford's other saint, Ethelbert, has survived.[46] The upper storey consists of an arcaded canopy which probably supported the *feretrum* containing the saint's remains. The arcading enabled pilgrims to insert their heads, allowing them to kiss the brass effigy of the saint on the middle slab.[47] One pilgrim, John of Holaurton, was witnessed

> placing his head within a certain hole adjoining the aforesaid tomb, and forming part of it; and when he had maintained the said head in the said hole for a length of time such as might be required to recite the Lord's Prayer three times, together with the Ave Maria, he withdrew his head from it.[48]

Other shrines

The great cathedrals and abbeys of medieval England contained the chief shrines to the saints, but scarcely a church in England was without its shrine, however small. These smaller shrines, at least in late medieval times, were more associated with images of the saints rather than with their relics. The laity left bequests in their wills to honour images of the saints with lights, and relics would have been found associated with altars in even the humblest church. According to the *Golden Legend*, in venerating the saints we pay 'the debt of interchanging neighbourhood';[49] the saints were first and foremost perceived as friends and helpers, and in an age when the doom painting over the chancel arch spoke to all of the wrath of God and of Christ's judgement they were very much needed to give encouragement and kindness.

Saints and their shrines came and went with fashion and political allegiance, and many saints' shrines were associated with geographical and historical accident. Often personal support for a particular saint was all-important. In the little Exmoor village of Morebath, the parish priest, Sir Christopher Trychay, had a particular devotion to St Sidwell, and on the very eve of the Reformation had made a splendidly painted and gilt image of this saint, to which devotions were made.

Each saint had his or her speciality. Barbara and Katherine were evoked for aid in childbirth and against sudden and unprepared death, Roch and Sebastian guarded against plague, Erasmus against intestinal disorders and Master John Shorne against ague.

St Birinus – saint of Wessex

The Venerable Bede claimed that the relics of Birinus, apostle to Wessex, had been placed in the Old Minster at Winchester. In 1224, spurred on by a desire to claim a prestigious local saint, the canons of Dorchester petitioned Pope Honorius III, claiming that they possessed the relics of the saint. Archbishop Stephen Langton was appointed to examine the case and it was decreed that Dorchester did, indeed, possess the relics – although the rivalry between Winchester and Dorchester, and arguments as to the veracity of the latter's claims, continued for generations.

The reliquary in the shrine was reconstructed in 1320 and this is described in some detail by the Chester monk, Ranulph Higden (d. 1364), in his *Polychronicon* – in which work Ranulph attempted to reconcile the rival claims of Dorchester and Winchester.[50] Certainly by then the 'saint' was displayed in a new shrine at Dorchester and this continued to bring in revenue to the canons until the Reformation – £5 per annum at the time of Henry VIII's survey of ecclesiastical revenue, the *Valor Ecclesiasticus*.

St Erkenwald – London's own saint

It was Erkenwald (or Earconwold) rather than London's first bishop, Mellitus, who became the principal saint of the diocese of London, with his cult focused on St Paul's Cathedral. A wealthy churchman, he

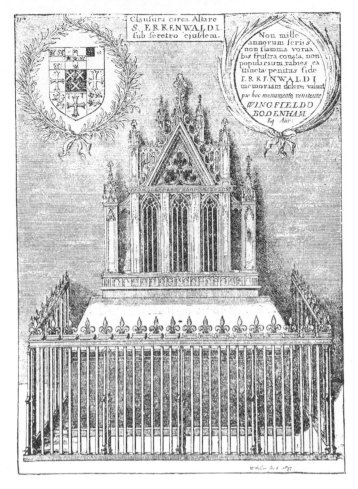

Shrine of St Erkenwald, from the plate by Wenceslaus Hollar, Old St Paul's

founded a monastery at Chertsey and a nunnery at Barking, where he died in 693.[51]

His cause was greatly helped by a group of miracle stories, dating from the twelfth century. His relics survived a disastrous fire in 1087 and were reburied in the crypt of the cathedral, where they survived subsequent fires in 1133 and 1140. There was a final translation in 1148, when the shrine was removed to behind the high altar of the cathedral. The cult is surrounded by story and legend. Once, when the shrine was in the crypt, a painter decorating the vault insisted on working on Erkenwald's feast day, even when people were coming to pray at the relics. The saint paralysed him as a punishment.[52]

In 1245, Dean Henry of Cornhill described the shrine thus:

The feretrum of blessed Eorcenweald is made of wood inside and covered on the outside with silver plates with images and [precious] stones.
It is said that the stones total 130. At the two ends of the same feretrum
are placed two silver angels with iron brooches: they cost 40s.

There was a final translation of the relics in 1326–27 and further
improvements were made in 1339 when goldsmiths worked on the
structure for a whole year.[53]

The appearance of the shrine was depicted by Wenceslaus Hollar in
an engraving of 1651. This, however, may be imaginary and it seems
extraordinarily narrow for a shrine of such significance. Erkenwald's
cult faded from popular memory following the Great Fire of London
in 1666 and no reference was made to him in Wren's new St Paul's
Cathedral.[54]

The Venerable Bede –
Durham's second saint

The bones of the Venerable
Bede were brought to Durham
cathedral from Jarrow in about
1022, and were at first placed
in the same coffin as Cuthbert. They were removed at the
1102 translation and enshrined
nearby. In 1370 the relics were
moved to the Galilee Porch
by Prior Forcer. The shrine is
described in great detail in the
Rites of Durham – a 'costly
and magnificent shrine with a
silver casket gilt with gold'.[55]
The present tomb, on the south
side of the Galilee Chapel at
the west end of the cathedral,
dates only from 1831, erected
following the opening of the
earlier tomb, as described by
the librarian James Raine.[56]

*Conjectural reconstruction of
the shrine of the Venerable Bede,
Durham Cathedral*

St John of Beverley – a saint for East Yorkshire

John of Beverley was an eighth-century archbishop of York. His life was documented by Bede, whom John had ordained deacon, then priest. He died in 721 and was buried in his monastery at Beverley. He was regarded as a national saint by 1000, and in 1037 was 'elevated' or placed in a shrine-like tomb by Archbishop Aelfric. The new shrine was 'of gold, silver and precious stones, of incomparable workmanship'.[57] There was a disastrous fire in 1188 and the shrine was relocated but the main trans-lation took place towards the end of the thirteenth century when the Minster church was rebuilt. There seem to have been two main focuses of devotion – the tomb of the saint and the shrine, which changed position as the church was altered and enlarged. The shrine was visited by many significant pilgrims, including Queen Isabella, who gave donations; she later visited again to make an offering on behalf of Edward II.[58]

St Aldhelm of Malmesbury – great saint of Wessex

Aldhelm was abbot of Malmesbury and bishop of Sherborne, a singer and a writer and one famed for his skills in administration. On his death in 709 he was buried at Malmesbury by Egwin of Worcester and his cult was described by William of Malmesbury – the reliquary was said to have been presented by King Aethelwulf of Wessex in c.837. It was embellished with images of the saint in solid silver and with scenes from his life and miracles.

In 1078 Aldhelm's relics were translated by Osmund, Aldhelm's successor as bishop, to a new shrine; at the same time, he removed a portion of the saint's left arm, placing it in a lavish silver arm-shaped reliquary, destined for his new cathedral at Salisbury. Osmund seems to have been attracted to Aldhelm's scholarship and his writings, and adopted him as his patron saint. His fame as a saint spread, and after hearing of various miracles Archbishop Lanfranc ordered that Aldhelm should be revered as a saint in his province.[59]

St Guthlac of Crowland – hermit saint of the Fens

Guthlac came of royal blood and became a hermit at Crowland, a site accessible only by boat, where his life, given over to prayer and silence, resembled that of the Desert Fathers. On his death he was buried at

Crowland and his cult soon became popular, with Wiglaf, king of Mercia (827–40) and Ceolnoth, archbishop of Canterbury (who was cured of ague), among its devotees. The feast soon spread through Mercia to Westminster, St Albans and Durham and eventually became general. The relics were translated in 1136 and the shrine embellished with gold and jewels. In 1196, Guthlac was moved again and the reliquary placed on a new marble shrine-base, supported on columns. It is in the context of this translation that we should see the magnificent Guthlac Roll – a series of 18 roundels – cartoons for stained-glass windows, based on Felix's *Life* of Guthlac.[60]

St Melangell at Pennant Melangell

One of the most engaging legends of a Welsh saint concerns Melangell (or Monacella). She was the daughter of an Irish prince, and in 604 she caught the attention of a hunting chieftain, Prince Brochwel, when

he was chasing a hare. As she prayed in a thicket, the animal took refuge in the folds of her garment. The chieftain approached but he and his dogs were struck with paralysis and his hunting horn stuck to his lips. Impressed by the young woman's piety – she had been living as a hermit in the valley – he gave the land to her as a sanctuary for nuns and hares. Melangell stayed for a further 37 years and became the patron of all hunted things, including refugees. Hares became known as 'Melangell's lambs'.

Melangell's remains were buried on the site of the present church, which dates from the twelfth century. The legendary site of

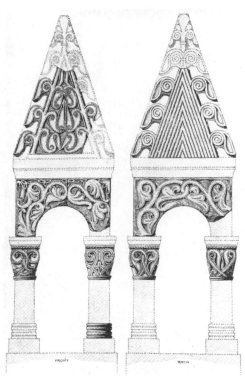

Shrine of St Melangell, Pennant Melangell, from Archaeologica Cambrensis, *1893*

the grave was within a small annexe to the main body of the church, known as the Cell-y-Bedd or 'cell of the grave'.

Our Lady of Walsingham

All the shrines so far described have focused on the body or relic of a saint and supported the great medieval fascination for and devotion to the prayers of the saints as communicated through their earthly remains. Shrines of the Blessed Virgin Mary were, of course, of a different order, as clearly there was no body to venerate; devotion was usually focused on an image of Mary, or a secondary relic. Britain had many such devotions to Mary but chief among them was the shrine at Walsingham.

Seal of the shrine of Our Lady, Walsingham

In the early twelfth century a noble widow named Richelde de Faverches lived in the village of Little Walsingham near the north coast of Norfolk. She venerated Our Lady and one day saw her in a vision. The Virgin Mary showed her the little house in Nazareth where the Archangel Gabriel had announced his joyful news and where Mary had lived when bringing up the boy Jesus. In the vision, the Blessed Virgin directed Richelde to note the dimensions of it so that she could build a replica in Norfolk.

With the help of village craftsmen, Richelde obeyed these instructions, creating a wooden house. Eventually, a stone church was built, 23 feet by 13 feet in size, around the wooden house, and her son Geoffrey endowed it with land. In the reign of Edward III the Augustinian or Black Canons acquired custody of the shrine and built a splendid priory around it. Walsingham rapidly acquired huge popularity as a place of pilgrimage – as 'England's Nazareth' it was able to satisfy the desire of people to visit a site closely associated with the life of Jesus but inaccessible in its original location in the Holy Land due to the danger of the Crusades.

Royal patronage of Walsingham became vital and monarchs from the reign of Henry III onwards made the pilgrimage to the shrine – Edward I is recorded as being in Walsingham on 12 occasions. At the heart of pilgrims' devotions was the statue of Our Lady, depicting Mary with the child on her lap. The statue is of later twelfth- or early thirteenth-century provenance and is similar in some respects to the statues of Our Lady of Rocamadour and Our Lady of Monserrat, both of which were carved at about the same time. Pilgrims came from all corners of the land as well as from abroad – those coming by sea disembarked at Lynn. So great was the number of those journeying to the shrine to seek a cure at Our Lady's intercession that the Milky Way was renamed the 'Walsingham Way', pointing, as it was said, the path to the Virgin's own house.

The Canterbury saints

Two ecclesiastical establishments in Canterbury housed a spectacular collection of saints' shrines and relics. St Augustine's Abbey contained the shrine of St Augustine while the illustration from Thomas of Elmham's *History*, reproduced by William Dugdale in his *Monasticon*, shows the large array of shrines surrounding the high altar.

At Christ Church Cathedral, the Saxon saints Dunstan and Alphege were venerated, but their cults were downgraded in a remodelling of the cathedral under Lanfranc, only to be restored to prominence in a subsequent remodelling under Anselm (1093–1109). Archbishops who were considered saints locally were buried close to saints of the universal Church – a distinction being made between those saints who were made according to popular acclaim and those who were canonized by decree of the western Church.[61]

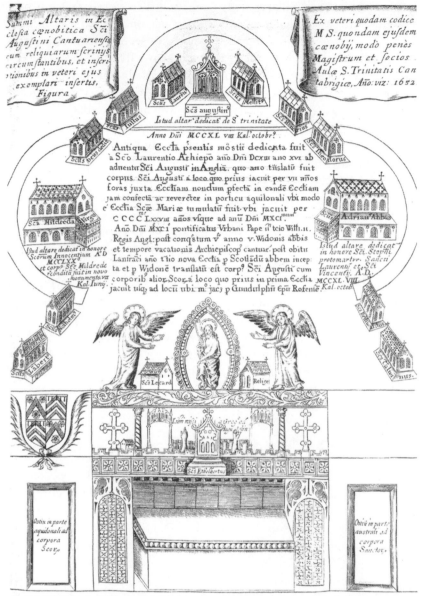

Shrines at St Augustine's Abbey, Canterbury, from Thomas of Elmham, History, *reproduced by William Dugdale in his* Monasticon

The Rochester saints

At the Norman Conquest, the local saint's cult current in Rochester was that of St Paulinus. Much of his episcopal ministry was as first bishop of York, in which role he baptized King Edwin at Easter 627/28. On the death of Edwin, Paulinus became bishop of Rochester, where he ended his life. His cult is documented in a book of miracles known to us through a fourteenth-century translation. According to this, Lanfranc personally paid for the translation of the bones of Paulinus, while other sources attribute this to Gundulf, bishop of Rochester *c.*1077.[62] Another early bishop of Rochester who achieved sainthood was Ithamar, who became the first Anglo-Saxon to occupy an English see; later he consecrated the first Anglo-Saxon archbishop of Canterbury, Deusdedit. Bishop Gandulf translated Ithamar's relics and there are recordings of many miracles at his tomb.

Near misses ...

There are several examples of attempts to encourage or start a saint's cult, which, for various reasons, failed to materialize.

Robert Grosseteste, bishop of Lincoln (1235–53), was famed as a scientist, theologian and teacher. On his death he was buried in the southeast transept of his cathedral, in front of the altar of St Stephen. When he died, 'the air was filled with strange sounds of bells and perturbations of nature'.[63] The bishop became the focus of a local cult and his successors and the Chapter of Lincoln attempted no fewer than five times to secure his canonization, without success. Grosseteste's tomb was built to reflect these aspirations – a tomb-shrine, similar in form and structure to that of Thomas Becket, with apertures for the devotion of pilgrims.

At Exeter Cathedral in 1943 a collection of wax models was discovered, deposited at the tomb of Bishop Edmund Lacey (1420–55). These models included human feet and fingers, animals' legs and hooves, and the figure of an entire woman, with attached strings suggesting that they were intended to be hung up – symbols of areas of the body prayed for or that received healing at Lacey's tomb.[64] Clearly, Lacey was the subject of a local cult, and while canonization never came this did not prevent local devotion. Instead, Exeter focused its attentions not on saints and shrines but on the liturgy; in the episcopate of Grandisson, the liturgy and the exultation of the role of the bishop within it became a defining feature.

At Hereford, too, there is an example of a saint manqué: Robert Bethune, bishop of Hereford. The period 1131–48 was the focus of a local cult, and by the fourteenth century there is evidence of a collecting box adjacent to his tomb for the gifts of pilgrims. Some of the miracles attributed to Thomas Cantilupe seem to have had their origin in aspects of Bethune's life. In any case, however great the enthusiasm for Bethune to be made a saint, this was soon quashed by the much larger body of evidence amassed in favour of Cantilupe.[65]

Questionable cults ...

Several saints' cults and their shrines bore witness to a less than appealing story and background.

In Norwich in the early 1150s, a new cult developed around a 12-year-old boy called William who had allegedly been ritually murdered by Jews in 1144. For the legend we are dependent on a contemporary, Thomas of Monmouth – and much of his evidence appears to be highly suspect, and anti-Semitic. The boy's body was eventually buried in the cathedral and placed on the south side of the high altar.[66]

A similar legend grew up a century later at Lincoln, where 'Little St Hugh' was said to have been martyred by the Jews in 1255.

Notes

1 See A. Herbert, P. Martin and G. Thomas (eds), 2008, *St Albans: Cathedral and Abbey*, Fraternity of Friends of St Albans Abbey, pp. 11–26.

2 B. Colgrave and R. Mynors (eds), 1992, *Bede, Ecclesiastical History of the English People*, Oxford: Oxford University Press, pp. 34–5.

3 See illustration, p. 8.

4 *History of Gruffudd ap Cynan*, pp. 124–30 in *Acts*, 234, D.7; quoted in H. Williams, 2012, *A Shrine Restored*, St Davids Cathedral, p. 4.

5 See F. Cowley, 2007, 'The relics of St David: the historical evidence', in J. Wyn Evans and J. M. Wooding (eds), *St David of Wales: Cult, Church and Nation*, Woodbridge: Boydell Press, pp. 274–81.

6 *Bede, History*, pp. 344–7.

7 J. C. Cox, *Catalogue of the Muniments and MS Books at Lichfield*.

8 See also W. Rodwell, 1993, 'The development of the choir of Lichfield Cathedral', in J. Maddison (ed.), *Medieval Archaeology and Architecture at Lichfield*, British Archaeological Association; D. Johnson, 1988, 'New light on the shrine of St Chad', in *Annual Report of the Friends of Lichfield Cathedral*.

9 J. Hewitt, 1876, 'The Keeper of St Chad's Head in Lichfield Cathedral', *Archaeological Journal*, 33, pp. 71–82.

10 J. Fairweather (tr.), 2005, *Liber Eliensis: A History of the Isle of Ely*, Woodbridge: Boydell Press, vol. i, p. 74.

11 *Liber Eliensis*, vol. ii, p. 79.

12 See D. Owen, 'Ely 1109–1539', in P. Meadows and N. Ramsey, *A History of Ely Cathedral*, 2003, Woodbridge: Boydell Press, pp. 67–8.

13 B. Nilson, 1998, *Cathedral Shrines of Medieval England*, Woodbridge: Boydell Press, pp. 37, 39, summarized from *Liber Eliensis*; see also J. Crook, 2011, *English Medieval Shrines*, Woodbridge: Boydell Press, pp. 155–7.

14 From *Acta Sanctorum*, see J. C. Wall, 1905, *Shrines of British Saints*, London: Methuen, p. 182.

15 See J. Crook, 1994, 'The Architectural Setting of the Cult of St Cuthbert in Durham Cathedral (1093–1200)', in D. Rollason, M. Harvey and M. Prestwich (eds), 1994, *Anglo-Norman Durham*, Woodbridge: Boydell Press, pp. 235–50.

16 See *The Rites of Durham*, ed. R. W. J. Austin, 1985, Durham: Dean and Chapter, pp. 68–9.

17 'The Life of St Werburghe of Chester by Henry Bradshaw. A.D. 1513, printed by Pynson A.D. 1521, and re-edited by C. Horstmann', 1887, *Early English Text Society*, o.s.88, p. 122.

18 See M. R. Newbolt, 1933, *St Werburgh and her Shrine*, Chester: Phillipson and Golder.

19 See J. Crook, 1992, 'King Edgar's reliquary of St Swithun', *Anglo-Saxon England*, 32, pp. 177–202.

20 See J. Crook, 2003, 'Appendix: The Rediscovery of St Swithun's Head at Evreux', in M. Lapidge, *The Cult of St Swithun, Winchester Studies*, 4, ii, Oxford: Oxford University Press, pp. 61–5.

21 See S. Ridyard, 1988, *The Royal Saints of Anglo-Saxon England*, Cambridge: Cambridge University Press, pp. 44–50, 154–75.

22 See Wall, *Shrines of British Saints*, pp. 22–3.

23 See J. Crook, 2005, 'The Physical Setting of the Cult of St Wulfstan', in J. S. Barrow and N. P. Brooks (eds), *St Wulfstan and His World*, Studies in Early Medieval Britain, Vol. 4, Aldershot: Ashgate, pp. 189–217.

24 See illustration, p. 24.

25 See J. G. O'Neilly and L. E. Tanner, 1966, 'The Shrine of Edward the Confessor', *Archaeologia*, vol. 100, pp. 101–54; see also H. F. Westlake, 1915, 'Notes on a recent examination of the shrine of St Edward at Westminster', *PSA*, 2nd ser. xxviii (1915), pp. 68–78; T. Trowles, 2005, *A Bibliography of Westminster Abbey*, Woodbridge: Boydell Press.

26 See T. Tatton-Brown, 1999, 'The Burial Places of St Osmund', *Spire*, 65th Annual Report of the Friends of Salisbury Cathedral, pp. 19–25.

27 C. Wilson, 1977, *The Shrines of St William of York*, Yorkshire Museums, p. 19.

28 See C. Norton, 2006, *St William of York*, Martlesham, Suffolk: York Medieval Press.

29 See M. H. Caviness, 1981, *The Windows of Christ Church Cathedral, Canterbury, Corpus Vitrearum Medii Aevi*, Vol. II, Great Britain, Oxford: Oxford University Press, pp. 180–92.

30 Caviness, *Windows*, p. 187.

31 See Wall, *Shrines of British Saints*, p. 160.

32 BL Cotton MS, Tiberius E.viii, fo. 278v (following the most recent refoliation of the MS).

33 D. H. Farmer and D. Douie, 1985, *Life of St Hugh of Lincoln*, Oxford: Oxford University Press.

34 Nilson, *Cathedral Shrines*, p. 13.

35 D. Owen (ed.), 1994, *A History of Lincoln Minster*, Cambridge: Cambridge University Press.

36 Nilson, *Cathedral Shrines*, p. 28.

37 Owen, *History*, p. 135.

38 See Crook, *English Medieval Shrines*, pp. 220–6.

39 E. Venables, 1893, 'The shrine and head of St Hugh of Lincoln', *Archaeological Journal*, 50, pp. 37–61.

40 Nilson, *Cathedral Shrines*, p. 160.

41 Owen, *History*, p. 181.

42 See M. Hobbs (ed.), 1994, *Chichester Cathedral: An Historical Survey*, Chichester: Phillimore, pp. 22–3.

43 P. H. Daley, 1982, 'The process of canonization in the thirteenth and early fourteenth centuries', in M. Jancey (ed.), 1982, *St Thomas Cantilupe: Essays in his Honour*, Hereford: Friends of Hereford Cathedral, pp. 124–44.

44 R. Finucane, 1977/1995, *Miracles and Pilgrims: Popular Beliefs in Medieval England*, London: Macmillan, p. 243.

45 Crook, *English Medieval Shrines*, pp. 235–9, 275–6.

46 See N. Coldstream, 1976, 'English decorated shrine bases', in *BAA Journal*, cxxix.

47 See R. Shoesmith, 1997, *The Shrine of St Thomas of Hereford – a Summary Report*, Hereford, p. 2.

48 Crook, *English Medieval Shrines*, p. 239.

49 Jacobus de Voragine, *Golden Legend*, see C. Stace (tr.) and R. Hamer (ed.), 1998, *Selections*, London: Penguin.

50 See H. Addington, 1860, *Some Account of the Abbey Church at Dorchester*, Oxford: Oxford University Press, p. 137.

51 See E. Gordon Whatley (ed. and tr.), 1989, *The Saint of London: The Life and Miracles of St Erkenwald*, Binghamton, NY: State University of New York.

52 Whatley, *The Saint*, pp. 158–61.

53 Wall, *Shrines of British Saints*, p. 105.

54 D. Keene, A. Burns and A. Saint (eds), *St Paul's: The Cathedral Church of London 604–2004*, New Haven and London: Yale University Press.

55 *Rites of Durham*, p. 44.

56 J. Raine, 1833, *A Brief Account of Durham Cathedral with Notices of the Castle, University, City Churches, etc.*, Newcastle: Blackwell, pp. 79ff.

57 J. Raine (ed.), 1879–94, *The Historians of the Church of York and its Archbishops*, 3 vols, vol. II, p. 343.

58 A. F. Leach, 1898 and 1903, *Memorials of Beverley Minster: The Chapter Act Books of the Collegiate Church of S John of Beverley AD 1286–1347*, Durham: Surtees society, nos 98 and 108.

59 See R. S. Cook, 1927, *Sources for the Biography of St Aldhelm*, Transactions of the Connecticut Academy of Arts and Sciences, p. 28.

60 See B. Colgrave (ed.), 1985, *Felix's Life of St Guthlac*, Cambridge: Cambridge University Press.

61 See W. Stubbs, 1874, *Memorials of St Dunstan*, Rolls Series.

62 See J. Crook, 2006, 'The medieval shrines of Rochester Cathedral', *Medieval Art, Architecture and Archaeology at Rochester*, BAA Trans., vol. 27, Leeds, pp. 114–29.

63 See Wall, *Shrines of British Saints*, p. 252.

64 U. M. Radford, 1949, 'The Wax Images found in Exeter Cathedral', *Antiquaries Journal*, 29, pp. 164–8.

65 Gerald Aylmer and John Tiller, *History of Hereford Cathedral*, London: Hambledon Press, pp. 217–18.

66 See A. Jessopp and M. R. James (eds), 1896, *The Life and Miracles of St William of Norwich by Thomas of Monmouth*, Cambridge: Cambridge University Press.

3

Shrines destroyed

The commonly held view is that at the Reformation shrines of the saints were all but completely erased from the religious landscape. Symbols of all that was hated in the medieval church – prayers of the saints, relics, indirect approach to God, wealth and prestige of religious communities – the shrines certainly provided a useful focus for the Reformers and made the English Reformation distinctly different from that on the Continent. There, especially in Germany, shrines were often spared. Luther himself saw shrines – and religious statuary – not so much as symbols of inappropriate religion but as beautiful objects that might, or might not, be useful to aid the devotion of worshippers. Thus, in Cologne Cathedral, the shrine of the three magi survives almost unscathed. Not so in England – the destruction was total – or was it?

The Reformation – destruction not wholesale

In the priory church of St Mary and the Holy Cross in Binham, Norfolk, is an extraordinary symbol of the ways in which the Reformation was implemented. The painting in the rood screen of Christ, the Man of Sorrows, dating from around 1500, has been overpainted with improving texts (c.1540–53) but now the earlier painting shows through – two approaches to religion seen side by side.

Earlier scholars presented a view of the Reformation suggesting a period of massive changes, in an England more than ready for Protestant ideas. To Arthur Dickens, the destruction of shrines, chantries and traditional practices was received with comparative calm by the population, as most people had 'ceased to believe in the doctrine of intercessory masses for souls in purgatory' and only a minority 'persisted in this belief'.[1]

Such views have been challenged in recent years, not least by Eamon Duffy in *The Stripping of the Altars*.[2] Duffy maintains that, far from being corrupt and irrelevant, medieval traditional religion was embraced by rich and poor alike right up to the Reformation. Prayers to the saints and the medieval emphasis on shrine and chantry gave them an invaluable construction to deal with the uncertainties of life and death – a construction that was demolished by Protestant reforms, causing great trauma among the population. The Reformation's emphasis on Word rather than Symbol would leave little or nothing from which the ordinary man or woman could gain comfort or encouragement. Medieval religion, in Duffy's view, was a vital adhesive for society, bringing together communities and ensuring, at best, a corporate and meaningful theology. Other scholars, like Christopher Haigh, insist that the English Reformation was not a joyous, national rejection of outmoded superstition, but rather a long drawn-out struggle between reformist minorities and the reluctant majority; rather than producing a Protestant England, it led to a divided England.[3] Duffy extended this further in his ground-breaking book *The Voices of Morebath*,[4] which helps us to see the Reformation as no seismic change imposed with uniformity and received promptly by a willing public, but a complex series of local adjustments, whereby changes were sometimes accepted and sometimes violently resisted – and where, sometimes, the elements of traditional religion were incorporated into radical new liturgies and theologies.

Cathedrals – business as usual?

If a great variety of practice was seen in the parishes, such variety was even more acute in cathedrals. On the whole, Protestant Reformers in England after the Reformation did not like cathedrals – relics of a catholic past. Thomas Cranmer had no time for them. He said of the canons of his own reformed cathedral in Canterbury that 'they spend their time in much idleness and their substance in superfluous belly cheer'.[5]

Others were equally dismissive of cathedrals and all they stood for. In John Field's 1572 *A View of Popish Abuses*, cathedrals are described as 'the dens ... of all loitering lubbers' where all holders of offices (including 'master treasurer, otherwise called Judas the pursebearer', and 'squeaking choristers')

> live in great idleness and have their abiding. If you would know whence all these came, we can easily answer you, that they came from the pope, as out of the Trojan horse's belly, to the destruction of

God's kingdom. The church of God never knew them, neither doth any reformed church in the world know them.[6]

In the event, despite the criticism they received, these great churches survived the reforms of Henry VIII – indeed, Henry created six new dioceses and cathedrals (Chester, Peterborough, Gloucester, Oxford, Westminster, Bristol), so we must assume that, for all their seeming representation of the old order, many positive aspects were found in them. Sometimes, like parishes, they embraced the new order; others dragged their feet and had to be brought into line through draconian measures.

In his important work on English cathedrals, Stanford Lehmberg has shown that, far from being places ground down by the Reformation, the life of cathedrals continued to flourish.[7]

Buildings were restored and developed and adjoining property for clergy maintained. Clergy numbers were maintained, too; cathedrals offered opportunities for many of the most able and fortunate clergy and provided stepping stones to the episcopate. Cathedrals continued as places of learning – indeed, the post-Reformation clergy were often great academics in their own right, and in the period after the Reformation many cathedral schools were extended and developed. In cathedrals of the Old Foundation (i.e. the non-monastic establishments like Hereford and Lichfield), even cathedral organization remained relatively unscathed and new sets of statutes tended to reflect earlier practice. Remote cathedrals often preserved their libraries, and former monastic buildings were converted to new uses. Music too, certainly by the end of the sixteenth century, was evolving into a highly complex art form again, after the austerity of the early years of the Reformation. With composers like Tomkins and Weelkes, the nature of English liturgical music showed itself as much more elaborate than that of counterparts in the Reformed churches on the continent.[8]

It is true that some elements of cathedral life diminished greatly. The hospitality given to the poor was now a shadow of that found in monastic cathedrals before the Reformation, and charity was sometimes given grudgingly.[9] Liturgical arrangements often led to hierarchical seating, with its emphasis on the gentry rather than on ordinary people, and some cathedrals were sparing indeed with their 'hours of opening', when compared with the years before the Reformation, when they rarely closed their doors.[10]

It seems, then, that cathedral life continued to flourish, albeit in a modified form. Areas of liturgical life were rehabilitated. Even altars, the prime focus of disagreement during the period of the Reformation, were reinstated, in wood rather than stone. In their work *Altars Restored*,[11] Kenneth Fincham and Nicholas Tyacke show the huge variety of practice in their area of liturgical furnishing and the fast and dramatic way in which such fashions could change. But at least the notion of the altar/communion table survived – as long as there was a Eucharist or Communion, then some kind of table was needed.

In cathedrals, then, we may expect to find elements of the more traditional. They were places of wide learning and antiquarian understanding; they had wider resources than most parishes and the presence of a 'team' of clergy in Chapter tended to provide checks and balances – more so than in parishes, where the parson's view could alone hold sway. Cathedrals, then are more likely to be strongholds of earlier practice and tradition. But might there be a big exception?

Chantries and shrines – the big exception to 'business as usual'?

In two areas of pre-Reformation life cathedrals seem to have found no way to rehabilitation – chantries and shrines. They are linked inasmuch as they are concerned with the prayers of the saints, purgatory and indulgences, and both struck at the heart of Reformed religion.

Chantries encouraged prayers for the dead and were often criticized as promoting a privatization of religion, although in many ways they bound together communities from all classes. While the practices of chantry priests and regular masses were casualties of the Reformation, at least the structures themselves seem to have found rehabilitation. Some chantry chapels became dwellings or schools; others were turned into almshouses or became private pews for the gentry; yet others provided space for elaborate tombs of the great and the good, where, instead of memorials seeking prayers for the souls of the deceased, they became monuments proclaiming their past virtues. From being places of life and activity, they became solely tomb-houses.[12]

Shrines likewise had a vital part to play in medieval piety. They provided a reason for ordinary people to enter the cathedrals – both monastic and secular, to pray and to seek healing. Their presence in cathedrals determined the kind of liturgy practised, and their presence influenced the staffing of cathedrals, with several clergy invariably responsible for the shrines and their workings. Shrines provided income for cathedrals – in several cases providing funds for major rebuilding programmes.

It is not surprising that shrines were so harshly dealt with by the Reformers. Buildings could be adapted to the new rite, music could now be set to English words, and income could, at least, come from other sources; but the shrines themselves stood for all that was most hated by the Reformers. They spoke of papal power, with their emphasis on canonization; they spoke of indulgences given by attendance at the shrine; above all, their theology spoke of the prayers and intercessions of the saints, in opposition to the Reformers' cry of 'justification by faith' and the soul's direct access to God. Even the papacy could, in one sense, be rehabilitated in the reformed English Church, with its focus on a high doctrine of monarchy and 'divine right of kings' – both emphasized absolute power in Church and state – but shrines spoke of purgatory and deliverance from it: all the elements of church life that Protestants were keen to play down.

And play them down they certainly did. The Commissioners' brief in 1535 was that monasteries 'shall not show no reliques, or feyned miracles, for increase of lucre'.[13] The returning Commissioners brought to Cromwell a stream of mocking reports and inventories of the contents of monastic and cathedral reliquaries, used to convict monks and clergy of superstition and pious racketeering. From Bury St Edmunds John ap Rice reported:

> Amongst the reliques we founde moche vanitie and superstition, as the coles that Sant Laurence was tosted withal, the paring of St Edmundes naylles, St Thomas of Canterbury penneknyff and his bootes, peses of the olie crosse able to make a hole crosse … with such other.[14]

Even while the Commissioners were about their work, they cannot but have been aware of the great influence these shrines had on popular imagination and devotion. Pilgrims often arrived in huge numbers while the Commissioners were on site. Richard Southwell reported from Walsingham in July 1536, during the destruction, that the offerings made there 'from the Saturdaye at night tyll the Sondaye next followwynge' amounted to £6 13s 4d, 'over and beside wax' – a big amount, clearly denoting large numbers of pilgrims.[15]

The most spectacular destruction occurred at Canterbury – according to one report the gold and silver filled 26 wagons, or 'the greatest collection of earthly treasure ever seen in medieval England'.[16]

On his journeys into Yorkshire Henry VIII would have seen widespread evidence of continuing customs associated with shrines. The traditionalist Bishop Longland of Lincoln seems to have shielded his diocese from most of the draconian changes and even the shrine of St Hugh in Lincoln Cathedral had not been demolished by 1540. Such actions led to a proclamation of the Privy Council on 22 September, expressing the king's displeasure that:

> Our good intent and purpose notwithstanding, the shrines, coverings of shrines, and monuments of those things do yet remain in sundry places of this realm ... the same being means to allure our subjects to their former hypocrisy and superstition.[17]

The bishops were therefore to begin with their own cathedrals and remove from them any shrine, covering of shrine, table, monument or miracles, or other signs of pilgrimage, and then to see that clergy did likewise in their parishes. Such proclamations were often assisted by strident preaching, especially from the friars – men like William Gray, famous for the *Fantasy of Idolatry*, backed up the official criticism of pilgrimage shrines.[18]

While the wholesale destruction of shrines had a measurable effect on the architectural landscape, there were also huge implications, theological and psychological, for the population. Although many English people were indeed convinced that the old church had played them for a fool and were glad of an opportunity not to spend significant amounts on intercession, yet for many ordinary folk the withdrawal of facilities at shrines demolished their only means of dealing with the huge threat of the afterlife.

In summary, while much of cathedral life would continue after the Reformation through a process of adaptation, on the face of it there seems to have been no room for the rehabilitation of the shrines. It could be argued, however, that they were the very objects that gave ordinary people 'permission' to enter these great churches. The shrines belonged to the people and were there to be prayed at and visited – by king and pauper alike. After the Reformation, cathedrals were no longer places for the ordinary people; they were inhabited by scholars, and in many cases simply became extensions of Oxford and Cambridge colleges – the worlds best known by the clergy who inhabited the cathedrals then.

Intrepid survivors

Shrines were highly dangerous commodities in the eyes of the new regime. Annihilations occurred in many cases, not least in Canterbury, where all traces of the shrine of Becket were ruthlessly expunged.

However, the Reformers' triumph was not nearly so clear cut as some historians would want us to believe. We read of pilgrims continuing to worship at Holywell in North Wales, at the shrine of St Winifride. Elizabeth I instructed the Council of the Marches (13 June 1579):

> To discover all Papist activities and recommend measures for suppressing them ... to pay particular attention to the pilgrimages to St Winifred's Well and in view of the claim that the water is medicinal to appoint two men to test its properties; if not medicinal the well should be destroyed ...[19]

Such proclamations clearly had little effect. A letter of 1590 suggests: 'They doe still goe in heapes to the wonted welles and places of superstition.'[20]

Visits to former shrines certainly continued in respect of Walsingham, and we read of the relics of St Thomas of Hereford being processed through the streets of Hereford in 1610 in an attempt to ward off the plague.[21] Recusants continued to maintain the tradition of the shrines. Relics were secreted for generations in private houses and brought out for veneration on occasions. Indeed, the extent to which relics maintained their power became known in the nineteenth century when huge collections came to light and provided the basis for legitimate devotion in restored Roman Catholicism.

Several shrines survived in the period after the Reformation. We now see three major examples of this survival – showing that the destruction was not as ubiquitous as sometimes portrayed by Reformation scholars.

Westminster Abbey – St Edward, the chief 'survivor'

In Westminster Abbey, the Confessor's shrine is a rare example of a shrine in which the saint's body remained relatively undisturbed. At the Dissolution, while Henry VIII was intent on removing all possible traces of the shrine of St Thomas at Canterbury, for political reasons, he was clearly more circumspect at Westminster, being reluctant for a king to be dishonoured when he was concerned to give prestige to the

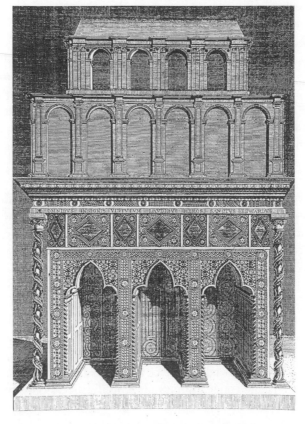

Shrine of St Edward the Confessor, from J. Dart, 1723

new Tudor monarchy. So, while the golden feretory was melted down and treasures seized, the saint's body was buried elsewhere and the structure remained almost untouched. Even the altar at the west end of the shrine was allowed to remain for a number of years.

During Edward VI's reign the shrine appears to have been dismantled, only to be reconstructed on the accession of Mary Tudor, when the Benedictine community was revived under Abbot Freckenham (1556–59). The new shrine was now clearly very different – the golden feretory had disappeared and gone for ever, while St Edward's body had now been interred in a cavity, hollowed out of the substructure itself. A new superstructure (in a debased Renaissance style) was clearly meant to copy earlier practice, but it appears to have been done cheaply and quickly.[22]

By 1560, 12 prebendaries had been appointed under new Elizabethan statutes, and these included the iconoclast John Handyman. In his time, while the shrine survived, its associated altar was destroyed.[23] But there seems to have been no intention to destroy the shrine itself. This could have been due to a continuing reverence for the monarchy. At this time it was still believed that monarchs could be touched as a cure for the 'king's evil' – a reminder of the mystical and magical surroundings of monarchy. This reverence was increasingly found in church buildings during the early seventeenth century – statues of James I and Charles I were installed in the neo-classical screen in Winchester Cathedral.

In Westminster Abbey itself, there was a great reverence for the royal tombs. The antiquarian Weever states:

> What concourse of people come daily to view the lively statues and stately monuments in Westminster Abbey, wherein the sacred ashes of so many of the Lord's anointed, beside other great potentates are entombed, A sight which brings delight and admiration and strikes religious apprehension into the minds of beholders.[24]

The churchmanship of Westminster Abbey in this period was conducive to the preservation of the shrine. Under Gabriel Goodman (dean, 1561–1601), the abbey maintained a fiercely High Church stance, with many pre-Reformation traditions continuing. Under James I, the abbey was revitalized as a place for royal display, emphasizing the Stuart kings' lineage and legitimacy. The public display of royal images, with new tombs for Elizabeth I, Mary Tudor and Mary Queen of Scots, reinforced this. It was all part of the growing tendency for Westminster Abbey to act as a kind of liturgical 'fifth column' showing what was possible in a reformed Church in liturgy and tradition.[25]

This reverence for the monarchy, especially as represented in the preservation of the shrine of St Edward, is found in the great eighteenth-century histories of the Abbey. Writing in 1723, John Dart places great emphasis on the shrine, with an elaborate and detailed description,[26] and a 1761 guide speaks with a typical hushed reverence: 'The first curiosity that commands your reverence is the ancient venerable shrine of St Edward.'[27]

Perhaps the most important evidence we have of the continuing importance and relevance of the shrine comes in references to coronation ceremonial. After the Reformation, there continued the tradition of depositing at the shrine during the coronation ritual certain pieces of regalia (the cope, dalmatic and royal vestments), while, at the coronation of Charles I in 1626, William Laud, bishop of St Davids, 'hallowed the cream' for the anointing near to the shrine.[28] Indeed, the whole area around the shrine continued, at successive coronations, to be a withdrawing area for the monarch during the liturgy. It is certainly interesting to note the extraordinary contrast between the decline in ceremonial in most parish churches and cathedrals as the eighteenth and nineteenth centuries progressed and the highly elaborate ceremonial associated with coronations in Westminster Abbey.

In addition to its relevance for monarchy and coronation ceremonial, the shrine seems to have received increased interest from other religious groups. Thus we find it as a focus for devotion among Roman Catholics in an early nineteenth-century reference:

> Such great sanctity is still attached to the shrine that a part of the stone basement seat on the east side of the South Transept, has been worn into a deep hollow by the feet of devout Catholics who occasionally attend here early of a morning; and who, from this point can just obtain a view of the upper division of the shrine.[29]

While, bizarrely, the following suggests the continuation of folk religion associated with the shrine – an amazing return to the excesses of pre-Reformation superstition:

> It is still, within the recollection of some aged members of this Church, that previously to the French Revolution, the very dust and sweepings of the shrine and Chapel of St Edward were preserved and exported to Spain and Portugal in barrels.[30]

The reverence for the shrine after the Reformation must be balanced with the forces of neglect that threatened to triumph on several occasions. Most famously, the tomb was damaged during preparations for the coronation of James II in 1685; the coffin was broken open and a gold crucifix removed and handed to the king.[31] Perhaps the most dismissive note is found in a reference for 1734, where James Ralph says:

> The enclosure behind the altar commonly known by the name of St Edward's Chapel has nothing remarkable in it, but certain Gothique antiquities, which are made sacred by tradition only and serve to excite a stupid admiration in the vulgar.[32]

The shrine was almost destroyed in the eighteenth century. During the 1770s, the dean consulted with his architect Henry Keene, together with James Essex and James Wyatt, about an 'improvement' that would have 'erected a new choir in the eastern part of the abbey, from the nave to the upper parts of St Edward's Chapel', involving the destruction of the altar screen and the clearing away of the Confessor's shrine. Mercifully, the scheme came to nothing.[33]

An early nineteenth-century writer bemoans: 'Once the glory of England, but now neglected, defaced and much abused.'[34] Another suggests: 'A few hardly perceptive traces of its former splendour exist.'[35]

However, by the middle of the nineteenth century, attitudes were once again changing and the royal associations of the shrine were clearly more valued. Writing in 1841, Charles Knight, viewing with horror the way in which the shrine was broken open in 1685, rages:

> If there were a tomb in the world which one would have thought an antiquary would have looked on with awe – ashes which it were a sacrilege almost to touch – we should have thought it was the tomb and ashes of the Confessor; around which hung all those associations; so solemnly and deeply interesting, however stripped of their superstitious alloy.[36]

In the shrine in Westminster Abbey, we have an example of a structure that survived the traumas of the Reformation, albeit in truncated form. It seems to have survived because of its royal associations, the protection afforded it because of its use in successive coronations and because of its symbolic value as representing a reverence for the monarchy.

Chester Cathedral – a shrine survives when put to another use

The shrine of St Werburgh was destroyed during the 1540s, but for a variety of reasons it fared better than many of its contemporaries.

In 1619, John Bridgeman became bishop of Chester, and with his episcopate began a remarkable series of reforms, associated with the seventeenth-century triumphs of High Church Laudianism. Laud and his followers were intent on a reverent approach to church worship and supported the renovation of churches and cathedrals which would enhance their worship. While dean of Gloucester, Laud had insisted on the introduction of altar rails, and Chester followed suit.[37] During the years 1635–37 there were considerable developments:

> Within it also he built a fair new pulpit, at the west end of the great cathedral ... he caused the stalls to be fairly painted and some of

them gilt ... he built the Bishop's stall in the Quire, Anno 1635 and gilded the organs in the cathedral and made a new set of pipes in it. He raised the steps towards the communion table and made the wall and partition there ... and he glazed the east window over it with the story of the Annunciation, Nativity, Circumcision and Presentation of Our Saviour.[38]

Of these developments, perhaps the greatest was the restoration of the bishop's throne, using the remains of the shrine of St Werburgh. Bridgeman appears to have taken the pieces of the shrine and placed them on the south side of the choir to serve as a platform for the throne itself. It must have been an extraordinary sight and can best be imagined by referring to the illustration.[39] The closest parallel would seem to be the

Shrine of St Werburgh, converted into a bishop's throne, Chester Cathedral

great throne over the tomb of Bishop Hatfield in Durham Cathedral, one of the few ancient thrones constructed of masonry.

Here, then, we have the extraordinary story of how one of the remaining shrine bases was viewed in the seventeenth century – not as a symbol of monarchy (as Westminster Abbey), not as an antiquarian oddity, not as something to be politely ignored in a Protestant Reformed Church, but as a structure worthy of being restored in order to exalt the office of bishop. The linking of sainthood and episcopacy was surely not an accident, and fits in well with an increasing awareness of the saints in this period – their influence on the Church and their role as patterns to be followed by those in positions of leadership.

While such high views of episcopacy hardly survived the somnolent years of the eighteenth century, the shrine/throne remained and no attempt was made to remove it. Indeed, when a further restoration was undertaken in the early 1840s, the shrine/throne was moved westwards by Dean Anson; in 1846 it was restored by Canon Slade as a memorial to his father-in-law, Bishop Law. In this development the shrine was split, the upper part becoming a high canopy, supported on pillars, with slender pinnacles added – an even more grandiose statement of episcopal power!

As a final note, during George Gilbert Scott's restoration of the cathedral in 1873, fragments of the shrine were discovered – fragments that appear to have been removed when the transformation of the throne took place in 1635. These were incorporated into the shrine base when it was moved into its present position east of the high altar, under the direction of Sir Arthur Blomfield in 1888.

Hereford – a shrine survives thanks to antiquarianism

If Chester's shrine survived in part because of its structure, several survived because of a greater level of interest in them as antiquarian oddities or items worthy of note.

The seventeenth century saw the rise of antiquarianism, as scholars became acutely aware of what had been lost at the Dissolution. The Society of Antiquaries was formed in 1586 and men such as John Stow (1524/25–1605) and William Camden (1551–1623) wrote major histories. A second generation of antiquarians lived in the period leading up to the Civil War, when looming conflict suggested that similar destruction to that at the Reformation might occur. In this period we should mention the work of John Weever (1576–1632) and his *Ancient*

Funerall Monuments,[40] and William Dugdale (1605–86), especially his *Monasticon*[41] and *The History of St Paul's Cathedral,*[42] in which he describes in favourable terms the importance of the former shrine of St Erkenwald – a courageous mention during the Commonwealth. This was the beginning of the age of the cathedral 'history', with detailed volumes written by Browne Willis (1682–1760) and Richard Rawlinson (1690–1755), who, in histories such as that for Hereford,[43] deplored the destruction and profanity of the Protestant Reformers. In all these histories there is a greater emphasis on the importance of tombs and memorials. This interest was popularized through *The Spectator* and Joseph Addison's other writings.[44] Shrines themselves became the subject of learned discourses, and we find by 1770 a Mr John Loveday of Caversham speaking at some length of different kinds of shrines remaining, focusing especially on the shrine of Cantilupe at Hereford.[45]

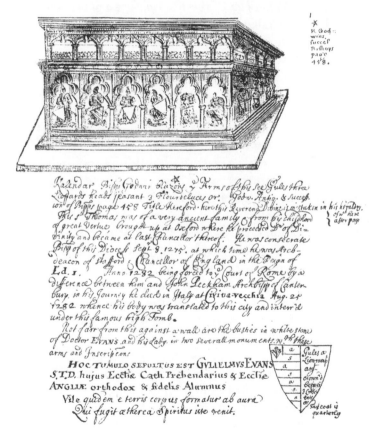

Shrine of St Thomas Cantilupe, Hereford Cathedral, from T. Dingley, 1684, A History from Marble

The shrine of Thomas Cantilupe (died 1282, canonized 1320) is a remarkable survival. The stone base dates from the 1280s, following the bishop's burial in the north transept. It is here that many miracles are reputed to have occurred in the years after 1285, in number second only to those recorded at the shrine of Becket in Canterbury – another Thomas, with whom he was often compared after his death.[46] In 1349 his relics were translated to a more splendid shrine in the Lady Chapel and it is this shrine that was destroyed by the Commissioners in the late 1540s. The relics were dispersed, some passing into the hands of loyal Catholic families, but the original shrine in the north transept escaped almost unscathed. The surviving shrine consists of two parts – an altar tomb surmounted with a stone canopy supported by an arcade of pillars and arches, the latter providing access to the relics for pilgrims.[47]

The earliest description we have of the shrine post-Reformation is in Francis Godwin's *Catalogue of the Bishops of England, since the first planting of Christian religion in this Island*.[48] A later historian, Thomas Dingley, in his *History from Marble*, gives a description of the tomb, 'whence his body was translated to this city and interr'd under this famous high tomb'.[49]

In the eighteenth century, Browne Willis writes:

In the great cross North Isle or transept, where is yet his Monument remaining, Consisting of an Altar Tomb, which had his Effigies in brass on the top of it ... he was After his death canonized for a Saint and many miracles are reported to have been Wrought at his tomb, as is described in his printed Life.[50]

As in all these accounts, it is subtle changes of wording that we have to note. Browne Willis makes more of the canonization and miracles – very much in line with what we know of his own beliefs and practices.[51]

With the rise of tourism in the eighteenth century, and the development of the Wye Valley tour, Hereford was visited more and new guide books emphasized the curiosity of the surviving shrine. Thus Samuel Ireland, writing in 1797, says:

Some monuments of their bishops still remain, amongst which, in the north wing is the Shrine of bishop Cantilupe. The monument of the family of the Bohuns, in the library is *curious*, [my italics] and deserved the attention of the antiquary.[52]

Increasingly, in the late eighteenth and early nineteenth centuries, writers speak of a residual use of the shrine by Roman Catholics – a glimpse at popular devotion unthinkable a century earlier: 'Many miracles were said to have been wrought at the place of burial, and the tomb is frequented by Roman Catholics.'[53]

Similarly, William Rees, writing in 1827, describes the shrine and then continues:

> The reputed sanctity of this prelate occasioned his tomb to be visited by pilgrims and travellers from all parts of Europe, and is still regarded with veneration by those who hold the tenets of the Catholics.[54]

We have, in the shrine of St Thomas of Hereford, a remarkable survival, and one that is clearly documented from the very beginning of the seventeenth century. Enthusiastic descriptions by leading antiquarians seem to have been partly responsible for keeping the shrine in the popular imagination. Moreover, as the nineteenth century progressed, we begin to see an even deeper understanding of the significance of the shrine – so much so that it seems to have attracted devotion from local Roman Catholics, a devotion which, while not shared by contemporary Anglicans, nevertheless seems to have been allowed by them.

The saints survive in writing and poetry

An interest in saints continued in the period after the Reformation and is confirmed not only in the survival of some key shrines.

The Laudian period saw the development of writing extolling the saints, not least in the work of William Austin, famous for his *Devotionis Augustinianae Flamma*.[55] Austin showed an interest in the relics of saints – most unusual in this period – tracing the history of an arm of St Bartholomew that was deposited in Canterbury Cathedral in the time of Cnut. He is sufficiently concerned with this relic to trace it to Norwich in the reign of Edward I via records in the Tower of London. Austin was not alone in his sympathetic interest in relics. William Prynne censured Bishop Richard Montague for urging (in his book *Apparatus ad Origines Ecclesiasticus*, published in 1635) that the relics of saints should be preserved and reverenced.[56]

Similarly, religious poetry of the period begins to extol the saints. The work of Richard Crashaw is full of allusions to the glory of the saints, not least the Blessed Virgin Mary, while a recently discovered work attributed to Thomas Traherne encourages reverence for the bodies and relics of saints. Here we have an example of an early seventeenth-century writer using language about the saints and their cults that would have been unthinkable only 50 years before. How attitudes had changed, and how 'broad' and in an all-encompassing way the Reformation Church *seemed* to be developing:

> In a qualified sense the very bodies of saints are held sacred by us and used venerably of us, being gathered to their fathers and honourably disposed of into quiet graves. For they were once the temples of the living God, whom nature teacheth us to handle with respect ...[57]

William Somner's *Antiquities of Canterbury*, dedicated to William Laud in 1635, shows an unprecedented interest in the history of the cathedral. Somner evokes the splendour of the cathedral on the eve of the Reformation. Recreating the pattern of complex worship in the cathedral, he imagines the chantries when they were alive with prayer, and recalls the throngs of people at mass; he takes us, in imagination, to the shrine of St Thomas, viewing it through the astonished eyes of Erasmus. The reader can have been in no doubt that the restoration of ceremonial worship in Canterbury Cathedral in the 1630s was deeply moving to Somner; he shows an intense sympathy with the pre-Reformation Church, and believes that religion should go 'splendidly dressed'. He makes no real protest against superstitious practices, such as the veneration of relics or the adoration of the Virgin, but accepts these practices as historical phenomena that have now ceased in England; there is no need to condemn them.[58]

Although writing later, John Marsham, in the Preface to Dugdale's *Monasticon*, very much agrees with the Laudian party, in deploring previous destruction and dishonour to the saints:

> Alas, we see the most august churches ... under the specious Pretence of Superstition, most filthily defil'd, and expecting utter Destruction. Horses are stabled at the Altars of Christ and the Relicks of Martyrs are dug up.[59]

The scene is set for a renaissance!

Notes

1 A. G. Dickens, 1974, *The English Reformation*, London: Fontana.

2 E. Duffy, 1992/2005, *The Stripping of the Altars: Traditional Religion in England 1400–1580*, New Haven and London: Yale University Press.

3 C. Haigh (ed.), 1987, *The English Reformation Revised*, Cambridge: Cambridge University Press.

4 E. Duffy, 2001, *The Voices of Morebath: Reformation and Rebellion in an English Village*, New Haven and London: Yale University Press.

5 D. Marcombe, 1991, 'Cathedrals and Protestantism: the search for a new identity, 1540–1660', in D. Marcombe and C. S. Knighton (eds), *Close Encounters: English Cathedrals and Society since 1540*, Nottingham: University of Nottingham Adult Education Department, pp. 199, 45.

6 Quoted in C. Cross, 1972, 'Dens of Loitering Lubbers – Protestant protest against cathedral foundations, 1540–1640', in D. Baker (ed.), *Schism, Heresy and Religious Protest: Studies in Church History*, Cambridge: Cambridge University Press, pp. 9, 231.

7 S. E. Lehmberg, 1996, *Cathedrals Under Siege: Cathedrals in English Society 1600–1700*, Exeter: University of Exeter Press.

8 See P. Le Huray, 1967, *Music and the Reformation in England 1549–1660*, Cambridge: Cambridge University Press.

9 Lehmberg, *Cathedrals*, p. 244.

10 Lehmberg, *Cathedrals*, pp. 213–14.

11 See K. Fincham and N. Tyacke, 2007, *Altars Restored: The Changing face of English Religious Worship, 1547–c.1700*, London: Oxford University Press.

12 See S. Roffey, 2008, *Chantry Chapels – and medieval strategies for the after-life*, Stroud: The History Press; see also A. Kreider, 1979, *English Chantries: The Road to Dissolution*, London: Harvard University Press.

13 G. Burnet, 1850, *History of the Reformation*, London, II, lxiii, quoted in Duffy, *Stripping of the Altars*, p. 384.

14 T. Wright, 1843, Three Chapters of Letters Relating to the Suppression of Monasteries, Camden Society, XXVI.

15 Duffy, *Stripping of the Altars*, p. 385.

16 See B. Dobson, 1995, 'The Monks of Canterbury in the later Middle Ages', in P. Collinson, N. Ramsay and M. Sparks, *A History of Canterbury Cathedral*, Oxford: Oxford University Press, pp. 69–153.

17 Duffy, *Stripping of the Altars*, p. 431.

18 See R. Rex, 2002, 'The Friars in the English Reformation', in P. Marshall and A. Ryrie (eds), *The Beginnings of English Protestantism*, Cambridge: Cambridge University Press, p. 51.

19 PRO Patent Rolls 21. Eliz. Part 7, quoted in C. David, 2002, *St Winifrede's Well*, Ceredigion: Gomer Press, p. 11.

20 *Archaeologia Cambrensis*, 1901, 13, in David, *St Winifrede's Well*, p. 11.

21 M. Jancey (ed.), 1982, *St Thomas Cantilupe: Essays in his Honour*, Hereford: Friends of Hereford Cathedral, p. 182.

22 See A. Tindal Hart, 1966, 'Dissolution and Revival', in E. Carpenter (ed.), *House of Kings*, London: John Baker, pp. 124–5.

23 Carpenter, *House of Kings*, p. 135.

24 J. Weever, 1631, *Ancient Funerall Monuments*, p. 41.

25 J. Merrit, 2001, 'The Cradle of Laudianism? Westminster Abbey 1558–1630', *JEH*, vol. 52, no. 4, p. 645.

26 J. Dart, 1723, *Westmonasterium or The History and Antiquities of the Abbey Church of St Peter, Westminster*.

27 *An Historical Description of Westminster Abbey, its monuments and curiosities* (1761).

28 J. Perkins, 1938/1940/1952, *Westminster Abbey – Its Worship and Ornaments*, 3 vols, vol. 2, p. 90; R. Strong, 2005, *Coronation,* London: Harper Collins, p. 248.

29 J. P. Neale and E. W. Bayley, 1823, *The History and Antiquities of the Abbey Church of St. Peter, Westminster*, London, vol. 2, p. 69, note.

30 Neale and Bayley, *History and Antiquities*, p. 69, note.

31 *Gentleman's Magazine*, 1817, p. 39.

32 J. Ralph, 1734, *Critical Review of the Public Buildings ... of London and Westminster*, p. 86.

33 Perkins, *Westminster Abbey*, vol. 1, pp. 131–46.

34 Quoted in Perkins, *Westminster Abbey*, vol. 2, p. 91.

35 Perkins, *Westminster Abbey*, vol. 2, p. 91.

36 C. Knight, 1841, *London*, p. 101.

37 D. Welander, 1991, *The History, Art and Architecture of Gloucester Cathedral*, Stroud: Alan Sutton, pp. 353–7.

38 R. V. H. Burne, 1958, *Chester Cathedral from its Founding by Henry VIII to the Accession of Queen Victoria*, London: SPCK, p. 116.

39 See illustration, p. 61.

40 Weever, *Ancient Funerall Monuments*.

41 W. Dugdale, 1718 edn, *Monasticon Anglicanum: or the history of the ancient abbies, monasteries, hospitals, cathedrals and colleagiate churches, with their dependencies*, London.

42 W. Dugdale, 1658, *The History of St Paul's Cathedral from its Foundation until these Times*, London: T. Warren.

43 R. Rawlinson, 1727, *The History and Antiquities of the City and Cathedral Church of Hereford*, London.

44 J. Addison, *The Spectator*, see edition 1965, D. F. Bond, (ed.), 5 vols, Oxford, pp. 108–11.

45 'Mr Lethieullier's Observations on Sepulchral Monuments', *Archaeologia*, 2 (1773), pp. 291–300.

46 Jancey, *St Thomas Cantilupe*, pp. 21–44.

47 R. Shoesmith, 1997, *The Shrine of St Thomas de Cantilupe – a Summary Report*, Hereford, p. 2.

48 F. Godwin, 1631, *A Catalogue of the Bishops of England, since the first planting of Christian religion in this island*.

49 T. Dingley, 1684, *A History from Marble*, ed. J. G. Nichols, Camden Society (1867), vol. 1, clvii.

50 B. Willis, 1727, *Survey of York, Durham, Carlisle, Chester, Man, Lichfield, Hereford, Worcester, Gloucester and Bristol*, 515.

51 Browne Willis spent much of his time travelling around the country, always attempting to arrive on the day of the patronal festival, showing his High Church/Roman Catholic piety.

52 S. Ireland, 1797, *Picturesque Views on the River Wye*, London, p. 51.

53 J. Price, 1796, *An Historical Account of the City of Hereford*, p. 97.

54 W. T. Rees, 1827, *The Hereford Guide*, Hereford, pp. 148–9.

55 W. Austin, 1637, *Devotionis Augustinianae Flamma or Certaine Godly and Learned Meditations*.

56 W. Prynne, 1646, *Canterburies Doome*, p. 211.

57 J. E. Barnes, 1970, 'A Caroline Devotion to the Virgin Mary', *Theology*, vol. lxxiii, pp. 535–41, quoted in A. Allchin, 1984/1993, *The Joy of all Creation*, London: New City, p. 116.

58 G. Parry, 1995, *The Trophies of Time: English Antiquarians of the Seventeenth Century*, Oxford: Oxford University Press, p. 182.

59 J. Marsham, 1718 edn, Preface to *Monasticon Anglicanum*, v.

4

The nineteenth century – shrines have a renaissance

We move from the eighteenth to the nineteenth century. If a few shrines managed to survive in the Reformed Church of England, there was little sense of their continuing use in worship or devotion. Any fragments remaining were essentially antiquarian oddities – examples of medieval stonework. For any development in their use we have to wait until the end of the nineteenth century. An important step on the journey was the involvement of the Roman Catholic Church in the discussion. This both hastened and slowed the pace of change in the Anglican Church. On the one hand, devotional practices embraced by the Roman Catholics were despised by loyal Anglicans; on the other hand, with the development of ritualism in the Church of England, what Rome had to say was listened to, in this as in other matters.

The Roman Catholic perspective – relics all-important

The re-emergence of shrines in England during the nineteenth century must be placed in the context of the re-emergence of the Roman Catholic Church from the penal days and its establishment in the mainstream of Christian thought in England. Penalties against Roman Catholics were removed by various Acts in the eighteenth century; the Catholic Emancipation Act of 1829 finally enabled Roman Catholics to take their place in society.[1]

The influx of immigrants from Ireland necessitated the speedy building of new churches, and by mid-century the Catholic population of the country had increased greatly. Full restoration of the hierarchy had to wait until 1850 – by this bishops were given territorial regions and cathedrals established in newly founded dioceses.

Key to an understanding of this newly emerging and triumphalist Catholicism was the emphasis placed on the saints – heroes of the faith, who had sustained the Church through dark, penal times. Eighteenth-century Catholics had played their part in this trend. Richard Challoner, the Roman Catholic Vicar Apostolic of London, published anonymously the two-part *Britannia Sancta*, a great celebration of the lives of the British saints,[2] while later Catholic leaders like Nicholas Wiseman and Frederick William Faber emphasized the part saints should play in the lives of English Catholics.[3]

The newly emerging Catholics were intent on proving their credentials as a denomination that had suffered during penal times. As a result, many martyrologies were published, emphasizing the suffering of the saints under the secular power. These were often key texts in the training of priests in Catholic colleges on the Continent during the seventeenth century, and this tradition of writing,[4] showing an anti-Protestant slant, continued well into the twentieth century.[5]

The saints, and devotion to them, were seen as central to the Catholic Church's full establishment in the land:

Oh yes, England is ripe for harvest, England will once again be an island of saints, She will be one of the brightest jewels in the church's diadem.[6]

This interest in the saints extended to an increase in patronal dedications of churches, chapels and schools, again emphasizing Catholics' 'ownership' and celebration of these saints, and led to a proliferation of devotional literature, with its emphasis on hagiography. The Oratorian Henry Sebastian Bowden offered a series for spiritual reading, arranged in calendar order, with each saint illustrating a particular virtue – Wilfrid for 'Devotion to Rome', Walburge for 'Devotion to Relics' and Gregory the Great for 'Prayer for England'.[7]

There was also a realization that this new, fervent devotion to the saints would result in an increase of anti-Catholic propaganda. The words of the sixteenth-century writer Robert Bellarmine were often quoted:

There is nothing that they [the Protestants] shudder at and abhor more than the invocation of saints, the cult of relics and the veneration of images. For they consider that these things constitute manifest impiety and idolatry.[8]

However, this opposition did not prevent the hierarchy from pressing on with this most important element of the restoration of Catholicism.

At the end of 1859, Mgr George Talbot informed the President of Ushaw College that he had seen 'the finest collection of valuable Relics that exists in the world in the possession of a private individual, and which he is obliged to dispose of by selling the Reliquaries'. Talbot continued:

> One cannot tell what blessings will accrue to England from the Relics of so many great Saints being transported there. Ambrose says that the possession of the bodies of Saints is a pledge that our prayers will be heard by them; therefore, I cannot help thinking that the Saints, whose relics you will possess, will redouble their prayers for the conversion of the English.[9]

The identification and cataloguing of relics, particularly of those of Catholic Reformation and post-Reformation martyrs, became of key importance. The Jesuit Fr John Morris wrote extensively on this subject, with his findings identified in manuscript collections at the Archives of the British Province of the Society of Jesus and in contemporary journals.[10]

St Thomas of Canterbury Roman Catholic church, Canterbury – shrine in the shadow of Becket's cathedral

As Roman Catholics grew in influence and confidence, they wished to celebrate the saints in tangible forms. In several cases we can observe the 'taking over' of a saint's cult from the neighbouring Anglican cathedral – a potentially antagonistic action, clearly showing to the world that a devotion, once practised in a cathedral but now defunct, could be legitimized and practised in a church belonging to a rival denomination.

The Roman Catholic church in Canterbury, situated in Bargate, is dedicated to St Thomas of Canterbury. It was designed by J. G. Hall of Canterbury and described by Nikolaus Pevsner as 'expensive ragstone N (ritual W) front, with a bell-turret secreted in a central pinnacle-cum-buttress. Mean sides.'[11]

In the nineteenth century there was a great deal of interest in the whereabouts of the bones of St Thomas Becket, and while much of this was purely of antiquarian interest, the newly emerging Roman Catholic community used it in part as an opportunity to re-present their own credentials as guardians of Becket's relics.[12]

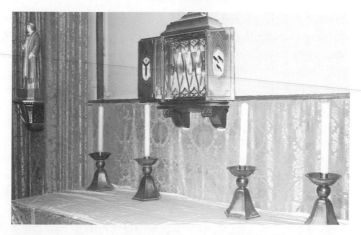

Shrine of St Thomas, Roman Catholic church of St Thomas of Canterbury, Bargate, Canterbury

The focus of the new church was clearly the cult of Thomas of Canterbury – even at the service for the laying of its foundation stone, in May 1874, there was an expectation that there would one day be a worthy shrine in the completed church to reflect that destroyed at the Reformation in the nearby cathedral. The sermon, preached by Canon Todd, expressed the hope that the glory of the martyr's cult would return to Canterbury, using less than ecumenical language and seeing the restored Catholic shrine very much in opposition to what was offered at the nearby cathedral:

> This was the scene of the labours of that great martyr St Thomas, who in that magnificent cathedral spent his blood for the principles of religion of that Church which was being so powerfully assailed at the present time. It was true that the cathedral still stood there, but it was like a body which the soul had left. Our Blessed Lord had departed from it and the ashes of the saint had been scattered to the four winds of heaven; and yet cold as it was, dead as it was, there was a lesson taught by the majesty and grandeur of the cathedral that could not fail for ever to teach a lesson to all who saw it of the truth, the honour and the dignity of the Catholic religion. They could not pray in that cathedral, and so they were about to erect a new house for the service of God where our Blessed Lord would be present with them.[13]

An appeal for the erection of a shrine, incorporating the saint's relics, was made by the editor of *The Universe*:

A restoration of the sacred shrine of St Thomas would lead to a revival of that piety which till 300 years after his martyrdom and till violently suppressed over 300 years ago, made Canterbury a place of pilgrimage, not only to Englishmen but to Catholics of all countries. Though a shrine is not necessary for a church, it is, it would seem to me, necessary for the new church, the only catholic church at Canterbury. If a chapel for each of the two other great saints (Gregory, Augustine) whose services deserve for ever to be remembered in connection with this place, cannot be aimed at for lack of means, the least that will content the good priest, I hope, is an altar of becoming structure in honour of each.[14]

The appeal for funds was successful and the church was consecrated by Cardinal Manning on 13 April 1875. Situated not 100 yards from Canterbury Cathedral, the new church indeed set up its own 'replica' shrine in a side chapel. Made of brass, it had representations of events in the life of the saints, especially Thomas Becket, embellished on it.

Later refurbishments of this shrine made a great deal of the authentication of relics placed in a reliquary above the St Thomas altar, and a further dedication took place on 7 July 1954, the feast of the translation of St Thomas of Canterbury.[15]

The fiercely anti-Protestant stance taken at the opening of the church and shrine in 1875 soon abated and the cathedral opened its doors to Catholic pilgrims, often supported by the publication of pilgrim manuals to assist in devotion.[16] Further ecumenical co-operation between Canterbury Cathedral and St Thomas' Roman Catholic church has ensured that the shrine of Thomas, for so long a cause of disunity and antagonism, is now, in both places, a focus of unity.[17]

St Chad's Roman Catholic cathedral, Birmingham – an audacious alternative

The setting up of a shrine to St Chad in the Roman Catholic cathedral in Birmingham in 1841 was an act both courageous and provocative. It was courageous as it placed the Roman Catholic emphasis on relics – a devotion always causing anxiety in most Anglican circles – at the heart of the movement for the re-establishment of the Catholic hierarchy in England and Wales. It was provocative as it set up an 'alternative' shrine to Chad's at Lichfield. Although it was one thing, as in the case of Canterbury, to provide such an alternative in a fairly modest Catholic

Shrine of St Chad, Roman Catholic Cathedral of St Chad, Birmingham

parish church, in the shadow of the great metropolitical cathedral, it was arguably quite another to remove that devotion 20 miles, from Lichfield to Birmingham, and to set up the 'rival' devotion in a new cathedral of the Roman tradition.

The medieval cult of St Chad is well documented.[18] At the Reformation, in common with other shrines, the main focus of the cult of St Chad was dismantled and the relics were disposed of. However, Chad's relics had a happier passage than many – those of the great Thomas Becket, for instance, were 'scattered to the four winds'. The turbulent history of Chad's relics during the seventeenth to nineteenth centuries is worth relating, not least as the story encapsulates the importance that the recusant Catholic community placed on the preservation of relics and how significant they became in the re-establishment of the Catholic faith. The finding and preservation of Chad's relics were, it seems, particularly important to the Catholic community, emerging from the shadows in the nineteenth century, as it gave authenticity to the Catholic church by using relics of its own post-Reformation martyrs; perhaps even more to the point, they were relics of a saint from the pre-Conquest days of the undivided Church.

According to a seventeenth-century source,[19] several relics were saved at the Reformation and by the seventeenth century had found their way into the hands of a Jesuit priest, Peter Turner. The box in which he placed the relics was discovered in 1658 by a party of soldiers and pursuivants who broke it open, smashed one of the bones in two and carried off part of the relics. In the early 1660s William Atkins, rector of the Staffordshire Jesuits, transferred the relics to a new box 'covered with silk'. In or soon after 1740 the relics passed from the Jesuits to the Fitzherbert family of Swynnerton Hall in Staffordshire. By a circuitous route, the relics passed to Alston Hall, near Stone in Staffordshire, and were discovered by a mission priest in 1839, under the altar in the chapel – a chest in which was a casket covered in velvet and embroidered with monograms in silver. The relics subsequently passed to Dr John Kirk, the missioner at Lichfield, who knew of their existence through the seventeenth-century Alban Butler manuscript. It was largely at the prompting of Dr Kirk that Bishop Thomas Walsh, vicar apostolic of the Central District, made a supplication to the Holy See, dated 1841, in which he sought leave from Pope Gregory XIV to expose the relics for the public veneration of the body of St Chad, 'of whose authenticity there is no room for doubt'.[20] Now removed from Alston, the box was opened and its contents examined by Bishop Walsh and his coadjutor, Bishop Nicholas Wiseman, prior to its final journey to Birmingham. The memorandum regarding the relics is written in great detail, worth quoting in full, and again emphasizing the importance with which these relics were held.

> Memorandum as to the relics of St Chad. St Mary's College, June 20 1841.[21]
> Die xx Junii 1841
> The box covered with velvet and lace in which the relics of St Chad were brought from Aston was opened previously to its being translated to Birmingham. In it were found the following bones:
>
> 1   A femur of the left side nearly entire.
> 2, 3 The two tibiae both broken at the lower end, one having the head of the fibula adhering.
> 4   A portion of the humerus.
>
> These four belonged to one body and are reasonably supposed and piously believed to be the relics of St Chad pursuivant to the evidence before us.

The relics were then encased in a reliquary designed by Augustus Pugin,[22] and the reliquary placed above the high altar.[23]

Contemporary accounts speak of the splendour of the Consecration service on 24 June 1841, and of the great authentication of the new cathedral in Birmingham, through their presence and cultic use.

On Sunday, the relics of the holy Confessor and Bishop, under whose patronage the church about to be consecrated was to be placed, were formally translated from the college, where they had lain for a few days, venerated like the ark of old, in the house of Obededom, and dispending, as is piously believed, blessings of similar kind to the united and happy inhabitants. A small shrine enriched the sacred treasure, which being reverently placed in a carriage, and accompanied by two ecclesiastics from St Marie's, proceeded to their destination in Birmingham. Here a much larger shrine, gilt and ornamented with jewels, was prepared on a bier, covered with a velvet pall in the Lady Chapel of the cathedral, where lights were placed around, which remained burning all night, while the brethren of a Holy Guild of St Chad continued until morning, with all the fervour of primitive Christians in the holy exercises of meditation and prayer.[24]

Between 1841 and 1963 the casket was removed and examined on at least four occasions – the emphasis on relics within the shrine still clearly of the highest importance. At some time during his episcopate (1850–88) Bishop Ullathorne opened the shrine; later it was examined on 16 February 1910, when Bishop Ilsley detached a few small pieces from the bones to be used as minor relics.[25] On 16 October 1931, Archbishop Williams removed one of the bones from the shrine so that it could be exposed for veneration in a reliquary in St Edward's Chapel, which was then being built at the north-west end of the cathedral as a memorial to Ilsley.[26] By the 1990s, there was a movement to authenticate the relics, and, by a decree dated 8 March 1993, Archbishop Couve de Murville established a commission of five members to carry out 'a thorough examination' of the relics.[27] The shrine was opened on 4 February 1995 and the bones delivered to Dr Angela Boyle of the Oxford Archaeological Unit. Radiocarbon dating showed that there was an extremely high degree of certainty that five of the bones dated from the seventh century and represented a minimum of two individuals – there are two left femurs. Three of the bones, it was reported, could belong to a man who lived at the time of St Chad, and could therefore be of the saint himself.[28]

The results of these tests were reported on 22 March 1996.[29] The relics were placed in a new casket and returned to the shrine above the high altar on 13 June 1996.[30] On the same day the archbishop issued a decree authorizing the continued cult of the relics, but as a group and not individually. The details quoted in all these instances serve to emphasize the point that the presence of authenticated relics in a shrine such as that of Chad at Birmingham was of enormous importance in devotion to saints in churches and cathedrals of the Roman persuasion.

We shall see, in the case of the revival of the shrine in Lichfield Cathedral, that the emphasis was on liturgical remembrance rather than on the presence of physical relics. The Birmingham Chad cult, although beginning from the physical, was soon supplemented with such acts of worship and remembrance, not least with the advent of a great procession through the streets of Birmingham. The pilgrimage/procession began in 1919 (25 May) and continued throughout the 1920s and 1930s. In 1940 the civic authorities asked that it should continue: 'at such times religious example would be all to the good'.[31] However, times were changing and the winds of reform blown by the Second Vatican Council found such expressions of devotion unhelpful – the last pilgrimage/procession took place in 1964, when Archbishop Dwyer considered the occasion reminiscent of a 'ban the bomb march' and discontinued it.[32] Alongside this, further devotion to Lichfield's saint was encouraged in Birmingham through the formation of the Guild of St Chad, but a more ecumenical spirit was fostered in 1922, when the first pilgrimage to St Chad's Well in Lichfield took place – an event that continued annually until 1933.

In the shrine of St Chad in the Roman Catholic cathedral in Birmingham we have a significant example of a shrine, set up in the classical Roman Catholic style, with emphasis on the proper housing of relics – relics seen as of vital importance in the re-establishing of credentials and spiritual authority. This 'taking on' of a devotion considered defunct in a neighbouring Anglican cathedral in Birmingham's case presented to the world the unmistakable message that the re-emerging Catholic Church was based not only on the blood of post-Reformation martyrs but also on saints of the pre-Conquest church.

St Etheldreda, Ely – a saint's hand gives authenticity

Ely Cathedral's patron saint, a doughty Saxon princess who presided over a double monastery of monks and nuns, was celebrated in verse by the Venerable Bede,[33] and her cult influenced the building and enriching of the great cathedral, not least the elaborate east end of the building, in which her shrine was placed together with the tombs of her saintly sisters. Etheldreda's shrine was particularly sumptuous and is described by Ben Nilson:

The surface of the shrine ... was of silver plate with figures in high relief, some gilded and some not, and set with beryls, onyxes, alemandines, pearls, amethysts, carnelians, sardines, emeralds, and one topaz. By far the most common stone ... was 'crystal' (presumably quartz) ... On the east side were two crystal lions, and other images, and the two sides supported sixteen figures each. On the western face were two images, including a majesty and a cross that was probably fixed to the apex of the lid.[34]

Etheldreda's shrine was destroyed at the Dissolution in 1539 and the cathedral rededicated to the Holy Trinity. Her shrine was destroyed in a particularly vicious way, for when it was dismantled the discovery that it was made of 'common stone' and not, as had been thought, of fine white marble, was trumpeted by the Reformers as evidence that the Roman church had blinded and corrupted the laity.

We shall see later the approach in Ely Cathedral to St Etheldreda from the nineteenth century onwards, but suffice it to say that it followed a very Anglican and muted response of remembrance, with emphasis on the life of the foundress rather than any emphasis on physical remains. This contrasts well with the approach in the nearby Roman Catholic church of St Etheldreda in Acremont Street. Designed by Simon Croot of Brampton, the church was opened on the feast of St Etheldreda, 17 October 1903.[35] In style and date, it bears comparison with the Roman Catholic church of St Thomas, Bargate in Canterbury, and indeed its 'rival' shrine and commemoration of St Etheldreda bear distinct similarities to the 'rival' shrine set up in Canterbury.

Shrine of St Etheldreda, St Etheldreda's Roman Catholic church, Ely

After the Dissolution of Ely monastery in 1539, the relics of St Etheldreda remained *in situ*, only to be removed forcibly by Bishop Goodrich in 1541, when he ordered 'all images, relicks, table monuments of miracles and shrines' to be desecrated and obliterated.[36]

As in the case of Chad and other medieval saints, some of the relics found their way into the hands of loyal Catholic families. Etheldreda's left hand was preserved in a separate reliquary, found hidden in a priest's hiding hole in Sussex in 1811.[37] This was subsequently presented to the Duke of Norfolk and passed to a community of Dominican sisters in Stone. It was found attached to an engraved silver plate, on which was written 'Manus Sanctae Etheldredae DCLXXIII'. The plate itself was of tenth-century style and suggested that the hand had been separated from the body in about the tenth century.

In 1876 it was reported that the hand had been found 'perfectly entire and quite white (but) exposure to the air had now changed it to a dark brown and the skin had cracked and disappeared in several places'.[38]

A small piece of another relic was passed to the church in 1950 by the church of St Etheldreda, Ely Place, London, while the principal relic remained with the sisters at Stone. This major relic was eventually given to St Etheldreda's church, Ely in June 1953, where it has remained since.[39] The relic is housed in a simple, glass-fronted reliquary in the church.

Saints emerge from the shadows in the nineteenth century – Anglican developments

The Oxford Movement is often considered to have reintroduced Catholic thought and practice to the Church of England – and in this we must include the re-emergence of devotion to the saints. Michael Perham, in his survey of Anglican attitudes to the saints in the post-Reformation period, reminds us that such renewed devotion did not emerge entirely in the early nineteenth century – the Book of Common Prayer made provision for saints' days,[40] and the so-called 'Caroline divines' showed a particularly high doctrine of sainthood in general and of the Blessed Virgin in particular.[41] Peter Nockles has explored the pre-Tractarian tradition of the late eighteenth and early nineteenth centuries, suggesting that this, rather than the Oxford Movement, led to a greater understanding of the role of the Church and to a limited development of ceremonial, not least in cathedrals, which are held up as places where ritual was often maintained in the midst of a bleak ecclesiastical and liturgical landscape.[42] But, without doubt, the Oxford Movement was highly influential in any move towards the highlighting of saints. Saints, according to the Tractarians, were not solely to be linked with the Roman Catholic Church, but had a long and venerable place within the Reformed tradition and as such should be celebrated. Saints now found new expression in Anglican liturgy and architecture – the emergence of Gothic Revival, 'ecclesiological principles', the Cambridge Camden Society and other societies firmly linked the Oxford Movement with a return to pre-Reformation practices. Such interpretations are found in many general histories of the Oxford Movement.[43]

Saints were celebrated through the retelling of their lives. John Henry Newman's *Lives of the Saints* (a collection of writings of several authors, following an initiative of Newman from 1840)[44] was paramount in this emerging genre, but received severe criticism as being too similar to Roman Catholic methods of hagiography. John Clark Crosthwaite, a London vicar, summarized these objections: 'Old sophistry, lying legends, forged writings, and the worst things of the worst defenders of the worst times and practices of irreligious popery'.[45] In other words, Newman seemed unwilling to differentiate between truth and legends, and in this way presented an approach far too close to Roman Catholicism.

Other writers preferred to emphasize the historical veracity of saints, rather than their devotional appeal – James Dimock wrote on St Hugh,[46] William Stubbs on St Dunstan,[47] and James Robertson on St Thomas of Canterbury, favouring an approach that used primary source documents and that played down any hint of hagiography.[48]

A new interest was aroused in national calendars, and we see this in the work of J. R. Seeley and Frederic Harrison, with their emphasis on 'worthies' and 'heroes' rather than miracle-working heavenly beings.[49]

The place of saints in the Book of Common Prayer became better understood at this time, through the introduction of 'Companions' – authors such as Celia Anne Jones and Elizabeth Rundle Charles looked back at saints of the past in a clear historical method but made it clear, too, that 'the saints and martyrs are not an extinct species'.[50]

Others saw the Celtic saints as providing a thoroughly British basis for celebration, offering a wholesome alternative to the post-Reformation martyrs now so beloved of the Church of Rome.[51]

Commemorations at the end of the nineteenth century gave opportunities for national reassessment of several saints, including both Augustine[52] and Columba in 1897,[53] while several high-profile historical pageants made great play of the English saints and their renewed place in the church.[54]

Cathedrals emerge from the shadows

If the Oxford Movement and other High Church movements enabled the saints to regain a foothold in the Anglican Church, the re-emergence of cathedrals – sites of so many of the medieval shrines – must also be recognized as an important context.

The Tractarians certainly held a high opinion of cathedrals and their place in Anglican ecclesiology. Gavin White has written that 'the Oxford Movement was obsessed with cathedrals ... because cathedrals were associated with bishops, who were the key to everything in the new ideology'.[55] But there is little doubt that the Oxford Movement itself was influential. Certainly, Pusey was thoroughly enthusiastic about cathedrals and all they stood for.[56]

But at the time when the Tractarians were coming into prominence, few understood what cathedrals were for.[57] They were perceived as places of privilege with little relevance to the mission of the Church of England. Reform was thrust upon cathedrals through the work of Commissions during the 1830s,[58] which redistributed incomes to places of greater need in the emerging church of the industrial north. The comprehensive work of Philip Barrett documents the major changes to cathedral life in the nineteenth century, in education, worship, church reform and building restoration.[59] He particularly highlights developments in ceremonial, which, although not directly influential in any development of Anglican attitudes to saints, does point to cathedrals gradually becoming places where such developments were possible.[60]

Cathedrals were also 'opened up' to wider influences, welcoming diocesan gatherings and reclaiming a specific vocation. Visionary deans and chapters published works that set out their aims. Among them *Essays on Cathedrals*, edited by E. M. Goulburn, was most influential.[61] According to one of its contributors, 'the primitive cathedral was the centre and focus of church work in the diocese'.[62] This stress on the cathedral as the mother church of the diocese was to be taken further in the work of E. W. Benson. He advocated the renewal of cathedrals by restoring the ancient relationship between the chapter and the bishop.[63] Some bishops actively encouraged diocesan pilgrimage – in 1873, Bishop Browne of Ely celebrated the twelve-hundredth anniversary of the foundation of the cathedral by St Etheldreda in 673.[64] Others seem to glimpse something of the potential for the tradition of saints and shrines in their midst. A. J. B. Beresford Hope writes:

The cathedral possessed obvious advantages over a mortal and trans-
latable bishop. Its potential was partly symbolic – in ancient sees, a
treasury of monuments to their collective history ...[65]

New railway networks made cathedrals accessible to large numbers of
people who travelled in search of history, art and music. Pilgrimage
was also being rehabilitated after its long slumber post-Reformation
and from its often unflattering association with Roman Catholicism.
Various pilgrim guides were published, which encouraged the practice of pilgrimage, emphasizing their antiquarian interest and showing
anew the extent to which medieval cathedrals had been centres of
pilgrimage.[66] The overview of Stanford Lehmberg puts it succinctly:

> All in all the Victorian era saw vast improvements in cathedrals.
> Buildings were restored, the standards of liturgy and music were
> raised, celebrations of the holy communion became more frequent,
> attendance increased, education was fostered, and crowds of tourists
> were accommodated. In many places, too, public campaigns to raise
> funds for the restoration and maintenance of cathedrals were success-
> ful and demonstrated a high level of support and affection.[67]

The views of Owen Chadwick, who was writing specifically about
York Minster, are similar:

> The Victorian Age was a high age for cathedrals. Railway lines made
> them the centre of their diocese as never before, and enabled them
> to satisfy all who travelled in search of history, or art, or music, in
> their relations to Christian worship. They had the beauty of the old
> ruined abbeys of the countryside, and were still a place where people
> said their prayers. England had money to spend, and all over England
> public-spirited men spent their money on restoring, building, decorat-
> ing, cleaning, adding.[68]

At this time, cathedrals were being restored and their opening services
often led to a reassessment of local saints – not with any intention of
cultic celebration but in order to celebrate them and make their lives
better known, as inspirations for dioceses and communities.[69] Indeed,
in referring to the dilapidated state of shrines at St Albans, Westminster
Abbey and Winchester Cathedral, James Stothert argued that it would
be better were they as 'other pious monuments of ancient times' to
be 'consigned to quiet forgetfulness, than that they should be com-

memorated with a scornful pity'.[70] His view would be echoed by many at the time, who wished to draw a clear distinction between Anglican and Roman Catholic approaches to the saints:

> In order to create a presumption at first sight against the whole history of the saints and holydays, it is only necessary to relate an occasional legend, which strengthens the incredulous in their disbelief in the narrative, and acts unfavourably on the minds even of those who are inclined to believe much.[71]

In summary, while Roman Catholic authors of the nineteenth and early twentieth centuries were emphasizing hagiography and the role of the martyrs in the emerging Roman Catholic Church, and, while this expressed itself in shrines that placed physical relics at the centre of the devotion, Anglican writers were emphasizing more the historical veracity of the saints and stressed remembrance rather than relic devotion. It is to the expression of that remembrance-inspiring shrines in Anglican cathedrals that we now turn.

Lichfield and St Chad – a shrine based on remembrance

While Chad, the great saint of Mercia, was being celebrated in the industrial city of Birmingham with a magnificent shrine containing his relics, Lichfield, his own cathedral and site of his medieval shrine, was adopting a much more sober and modest approach to the celebration of his memory.

Lichfield Cathedral was restored in two main phases during the nineteenth century, 1854–61 and 1876–83. In both of these restorations, opportunity was taken to raise the profile of St Chad as patron saint of cathedral and diocese. The emphasis was very much on pilgrimage. In a sermon on the cathedral's restoration in 1860, G. H. Curteis, Principal of Lichfield Theological College, saw the cathedral as 'a place to which pilgrimage may once more be made, not now in superstition, but in search of that which, however denied, human nature can never cease to crave – tranquil beauty and religious peace'.[72] Thus, devotion to Chad was made, essentially, not at the site of the shrine but through new depictions of the saint, which served to inform the visitor and worshipper of aspects of his life rather than as a focus for veneration. There are many new images of Chad in various parts of the cathedral – works of stained glass, sculptures on the west front and at the north

Victorian roundel of St Chad in Choir, Lichfield Cathedral

transept entrance, a statue in the font niche and scenes from his life on the chancel pavement medallions.[73] Chad is seen not so much as a physical presence to be venerated but as a vitally important figure in the Church of the seventh century, who has important things to say to this generation. Thus in the 1895 Lonsdale window by Kempe he is interpreted as an agent of unity between the Anglian and Mercian churches, and also as one who looks forward to other key saints in the English tradition – Boniface, Wulfstan and Hugh. Various sermons of this period press home the point of Chad's importance – H. E. Savage exhorted the diocese to see Chad's cathedral as 'a rallying point of patriotism',[74] while the annual St Chad's day lecture, instituted in 1913, gave opportunities of celebrating the saint's life and ministry.[75]

As to the physical remnants of the medieval cult, at first more attention was paid not to the site of the shrine itself but to the Chapel of St Chad's Head, built during the fourteenth century, with its gallery to display relics to pilgrims. By the end of the nineteenth century, the chapel was in a parlous state of repair, but thanks to the efforts of Dean Lucock (dean 1892–1909), it was restored and contains references to the saint throughout – especially corbels and stained glass. The chapel was rededicated on St Chad's day 1897, when services were attended by the mayor and corporation and a lunch served to 200 clergy.[76]

The emphasis on remembrance of Chad's life continued under Dean Savage, who, in addition to his institution of the annual St Chad's day lecture, began, in 1912, the custom of reading out names of benefactors as well as providing a collect and readings for use on Chad's feast day.[77]

Ely Cathedral and St Etheldreda – muted remembrance

While the Roman Catholic church in Ely, in common with other examples at Canterbury and Birmingham, emphasizes the presence of the physical remains of St Etheldreda, enshrined within the building, only 200 yards away Ely Cathedral adopts a different and more 'Anglican' approach.

The cathedral's rediscovery of the shrine of its foundress and saint, Etheldreda, follows something of the pattern we have seen in Lichfield's remodelling of devotion of St Chad, with an emphasis on a renewed remembering of the attributes of the saint rather than any physical reconstruction of the medieval shrine.

At the Reformation, all physical reminders of St Etheldreda were removed from the cathedral, although medieval carvings, out of reach of the Reformers' hammers, survived.[78] However, the cathedral did not entirely forget Etheldreda in the post-Reformation period – the eighteenth-century remodelling of the cathedral (which necessitated the removal in 1769 of the 'Saxon Confessors' from the north of the then choir, in the octagon, to their present resting place in Bishop West's chapel) revived antiquarian interest. A small full-length depiction of Etheldreda, removed from Ely House, Holborn to Ely Palace for safe-keeping by Bishop Mawson, attracted the interest of William Cole, who sent Horace Walpole a sketch of it in 1762; it was later placed in the middle lancet of the east window.[79] It is now at the head of the window in the chapel of St Dunstan and St Ethelwold. Antiquarian interest in the shrine itself was further influenced through the writings of the cathedral's eighteenth-century historian, James Bentham, who wrote in disparaging terms of the use of the shrine, when describing the choir of the cathedral:

This stately and sumptuous part of the Fabrick was built in order to extend the Church to a more convenient length for the reception of the High Altar, but particularly to make room for the magnificent

Shrine of St Etheldreda, and for such-like gainful and superstitious purposes; therefore of course fell into disuse after the Reformation: and was in a manner lost, or an useless incumbrance to the Church ...[80]

The cathedral's interest in St Etheldreda appears to have been revived by Dean Charles Merivale for the celebration in 1873 of the bi-sexcentenary of the foundation of the monastery. In the preface to his published account of the festival, Merivale notes:

> The 17th day of October is still marked in our Ecclesiastical Calendar as the Festival of Etheldreda, Virgin and Queen, the foundress and first abbess ... our Reformers would no doubt have swept away all remembrance of them [the stories of Etheldreda], had not the great Fair which is still held at Ely been connected with the anniversary of the translation.[81]

However, Dean Merivale was himself clearly uncomfortable with the idea of Etheldreda as a saint, and referred to her throughout his sermon as 'Queen Etheldreda', preferring her as a royal foundress rather than a canonized saint. In this he was not alone: throughout the sermons delivered over the four days of the 1873 festival, the figure of Etheldreda seemed to disquiet the speakers, through her rather chequered career in two celibate marriages. Sabine Baring-Gould had spoken of her as one who 'kindled an answering flame' in Wilfrid's 'cold breast' – something of a Saxon *femme fatale*![82]

In Ely Cathedral we have an example of a modest restoration of devotion to the patron saint, focused not so much on the physical remains but on annual remembrances, with understated pointers to the site of the pre-Reformation shrine itself.

St Albans – the first reinvention of a saint's shrine

After the destruction of the shrine of St Alban in the 1530s, the abbey church continued as a parish church for the town and very little was made of the saint in whose honour the church was built.

In 1847, Dr Nicholson, Rector of St Albans Abbey, while involved in some repair work, found several pieces of carved Purbeck marble, which he believed to have formed part of the shrine of St Alban. No further search was made at the time, but Dr Nicholson was proved

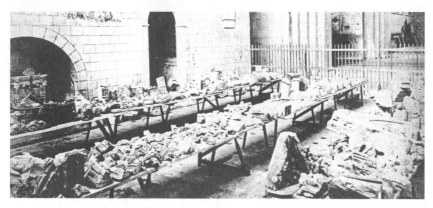

Over 2,000 pieces of the shrines of St Alban and St Amphibalus were discovered when the wall between the Lady Chapel and the shrine area was demolished in 1872. Here they are laid out in the south transept prior to reassembly

right when in 1872 work began to open up the blocked arches in the eastern arm of the church and a great discovery was made. Much of the rubble from the arches was found to be pieces of carved and painted Purbeck marble, fragments of which were surely the long-lost shrine of the saint. Beautifully carved limestone fragments also appeared,

Shrine of St Alban as reassembled in 1872

thought by George Gilbert Scott to belong to the destroyed shrine of St Amphibalus. The discovery made the national newspapers. The fragments – over 2,000 of them – were reassembled under the guidance of John Chapple, Clerk of Works to Scott, although there was much criticism from Low Church members of the restoration committee! When John Ruskin heard of this criticism, he silenced critics by offering to pay for these restorations himself.

Shrine of St Amphibalus as reassembled in 1872

Reconstructed, the shrine stood for a century, a tribute to Victorian skill and ingenuity, but by the 1990s was becoming increasingly insecure.[83]

Notes

1 O. Chadwick, 1966/1971, *The Victorian Church*, Vol. 1, London: Adam and Charles Black, p. 271.

2 R. Challoner, 1745, *Britannia Sancta: or, the Lives of the most celebrated British, English, Scottish, and Irish Saints: who have flourished in these islands, from the earliest times of Christianity, down to the change of religion in the sixteenth century, faithfully collected from their ancient acts, and other records of British history*, London.

3 N. Wiseman, 1853, 'On National Holydays', in *Essays on various subjects by His Eminence Cardinal Wiseman*, London: Charles Dolman; F. W. Faber, 1853, *The Life of S. Francis of Assisi, with an essay on the characteristics of the lives of the saints*, London: Richardson & Son.

4 J. Wilson, 1970, *The English Martyrologie 1608*, Amsterdam, New York: Da Capo Press.

5 1838, *Modern British Martyrology*, London: Thomas Jones; J. H. Pollen, 1891, *Acts of English Martyrs*, London: Burns and Oates; R. Stanton, 1892, *A Menology of England and Wales*, London: Burns and Oates.

6 Ambrose Phillipps to Cardinal Acton, 1842, in E. S. Purcell, 1900, *Life and Letters of Ambrose Phillipps de Lisle*, London, New York: Macmillan, i.237.

7 H. S. Bowden (ed.), 1877, *Miniature lives of the saints for every day in the year*, 2nd edn, London: Burns and Oates.

8 R. Bellarmine, 1601, *De controversiis Christiane fidei*, Ingolstadt, ii, p. 821.

9 *Catalogue of the Collection of Relics belonging to St Cuthbert's College, Ushaw*, 1881, Preston, pp. 6–8.

10 See J. Morris, 1888, *The Relics of St Thomas of Canterbury*, Canterbury: Hal Drury; J. R. Butler, 1996, *The Quest for Becket's Bones: The Mystery of the Relics of St Thomas of Canterbury*, New Haven, CT and London: Yale University Press; J. Morris, 'English Relics – St Thomas of Hereford', *The Month*, 1882, pp. 112–16; J. Morris, 'The English Martyrs', *The Month*, January 1887, p. 7; J. Morris, 'The English Martyrs, known and unknown', *The Month*, April 1887, pp. 534–7.

11 J. Newman, 1969, *The Buildings of England – North East and East Kent*, London: Penguin, p. 245; N. Mayhew Smith, 2010, *Britain's Holiest Places*, Bristol: Lifestyle Press, pp. 38–9.

12 1888, *An Anatomical Report on the skeleton found by Mr Pugin Thornton*, Canterbury: E. Crow.

13 *Kentish Gazette*, 19 May 1874.

14 Letter to Editor, *The Universe*, 18 March 1874.

15 A pamphlet on the history of St Thomas of Canterbury RC church describes the provenance of the various relics. On one case is a small piece of vestment and a small piece of bone of St Thomas. These relics are reported as coming from Italy, with a certificate of authentication, dated 14 October 1794, issued by Bishop Octavius Angelelli of Gubbio. Subsequent certificates of authentication were issued by Cardinal Wiseman (17 July 1863) and by Cardinal Bourne (1 June 1926). The other case contains a piece of bone, 2½ inches long. This relic was, with others of St Thomas, in the Cistercian house of Pontigny (where St Thomas stayed in his years of exile). From the abbey it passed to the bishop of Tournai, who eventually gave it to the Benedictine Abbey at Chevetogne. Through Fr Thomas Becquet OSB this relic was brought to England and presented to the local bishop (of Southwark) who deposited it in Canterbury.

16 J. Morris, 1889, *Canterbury: Our old metropolis*, Canterbury: E. Crow; Anon, n.d., *Canterbury: A Guide for Catholics – a step-by-step guide to the cathedral, describing shrines of Alphege, Dunstan, Thomas*.

17 From 1969, Roman Catholic masses have been permitted in Canterbury Cathedral; in 1975 the dean of Canterbury attended mass at St Thomas' church as part of the centenary celebrations; in February 1978, it was agreed that the

Roman Catholic parish of St Thomas might hold two masses in the cathedral each year and that large pilgrimages might hold masses in the eastern crypt; in 1979, the Roman Catholic archbishop of Southwark agreed to preach during the octave of prayer for Christian Unity.

18 W. Rodwell, 1993, 'The development of the Choir of Lichfield Cathedral', in J. Maddison (cd.), *Medieval Archaeology and Architecture at Lichfield*, British Archaeological Assn; D. Johnson, 1988, 'New light on the shrine of St Chad', in *Annual Report of the Friends of Lichfield Cathedral*, pp. 11–12; J. Crook, 2011, *English Medieval Shrines*, Woodbridge: Boydell Press, pp. 33, 64–5, 220, 295, 304.

19 Birmingham Archdiocesan Archives (BAA), MS. 'Alban Butler's Collection for Bp Chaloner's [sic] Lives of Missionary Priests. Given me [Dr Kirk] by Charles Butler Esq.', pp. 49–52. A slightly altered version is printed by H. Foley, *Records of the English Province of the Society of Jesus*, ii, 231–2, with a translation of the Latin in iii, pp. 794–7.

20 BAA P1/51/7, 'Relazione di Udienza SSma 17 Maggio 1841 Inghilterra'.

21 BAA P1/51/4.

22 P. Atterbury and C. Wainwright (eds), 1994, *Pugin: A Gothic Passion*, Newhaven and London: Yale University Press, p. 73 and fig. 134; R. Hill, 2008, *God's Architect: Pugin and the Building of Romantic Britain*, London: Penguin, pp. 208–11.

23 M. W. Greenslade, 1996, *Saint Chad of Lichfield and Birmingham*, Archdiocese of Birmingham Historical Commission, publication no. 10, p. 18.

24 *The Tablet*, no. LIX, 26 June, 1841, p. 413.

25 *St Chad's Magazine*, March 1910, pp. 1–3.

26 J. Sharp, 2000, 'The Relics of Saint Chad', *Midland Catholic History*, no. 7, p. 2.

27 Greenslade, *Saint Chad*, p. 3.

28 A. Boyle,1998, 'The bones of the Anglo-Saxon bishop and saint, Chad: a scientific analysis', *Church Archaeology*, ii, pp. 35–8.

29 Archives of the Archbishop of Birmingham, File on St Chad's Relics Commission: Canon Law Process, transcript, 22 March 1996.

30 Archives transcript, 13 June 1996.

31 Greenslade, *Saint Chad*, p. 19.

32 Greenslade, *Saint Chad*, p. 20.

33 B. Colgrave and R. Mynors (eds), 1992, *Bede, Ecclesiastical History of the English People*, Oxford: Oxford University Press, iv, 19–20, pp. 390–401.

34 B. Nilson, 1977/1995, *Cathedral Shrines of Medieval England*, Woodbridge: Boydell Press, pp. 37, 39.

35 N. Pevsner, 1987, *The Buildings of England – Cambridgeshire*, London: Penguin, p. 380; P. Bright, 1987, *A History of the Catholic Church of St Etheldreda in Ely*, private publication, p. 2.

36 C. W. Stubbs, 1867, *Historical Memorials of Ely Cathedral*, London: J. M. Dent, p. 42.

37 Bright, *History*, p. 42.

38 A. Wood, 2 March 1876, 'St Etheldreda and her churches in Ely and London: A preliminary notice of Catholic Memorials in the vicinity of the latter

and a Supplementary Account of Ely House', lecture at St Etheldreda, Ely Place. Papers in the Cambridgeshire Collection, C52, p. 16.

39 Wood, 'St Etheldreda', p. 9.

40 M. Perham, 1979, *The Communion of Saints*, London: Alcuin Club/SPCK, pp. 62–6.

41 See A. M. Allchin, 1984/1993, *The Joy of all Creation*, London: New City, pp. 107–35.

42 P. B. Nockles, 2008, 'The Oxford Movement as Religious Revival and Resurgence', in K. Cooper and J. Gregory (eds), *Revival and Resurgence in Christian History*, Woodbridge: Boydell Press; P. B. Nockles, 1994, *The Oxford Movement in Context: Anglican High Churchmanship 1760–1857*, Cambridge: Cambridge University Press.

43 M. Chandler, 2003, *An Introduction to the Oxford Movement*, London: SPCK; O. Chadwick, 1990, *The Spirit of the Oxford Movement*, Cambridge: Cambridge University Press.

44 A. W. Hutton, 1901, *The Lives of the English Saints written by various hands at the suggestion of John Henry Newman, afterwards Cardinal*, London: S. T. Freemantle.

45 *British Magazine*, 28 (October 1845), p. 364.

46 J. F. Dimock (ed.), 1864, *Magna Vita S.Hugonis Episcopi Lincolnensis, from manuscripts in the Bodleian Library, Oxford, and the Imperial Library, Paris*, London: Longman, Green, Longman, Roberts & Green.

47 W. Stubbs (ed.), 1847, *Memorials of Saint Dunstan, Archbishop of Canterbury edited from various manuscript sources*, London: Longman.

48 J. C. Robertson (ed.), 1876, *Materials for the History of Thomas Becket, Archbishop of Canterbury (Canonized by Pope Alexander III, AD 1173)*, London: Longman.

49 F. Harrison (ed.), 1892, *The new calendar of great men: Biographies of the 338 worthies of all ages and nations in the Positivist calendar of Auguste Comte*, London, New York: Macmillan.

50 C. A. Jones, n.d. [1871], *The Saints of Old: Being short sketches of the Holy-Days found in the Kalendar of the English Church*, London: J. T. Hayes; E. R. Charles, 1887, *Martyrs and Saints of the First Twelve Centuries: Studies in the lives of the black letter saints of the English calendar*, London: SPCK.

51 S. Baring-Gould, 1872, *The Lives of the Saints*, 2nd edn, London: John Hodges.

52 W. E. Collins, 'The coming of St Augustine', part 2, *Church Times*, 14 May 1897, p. 582.

53 'Iona Correspondent', *Church Times*, 2 July 1897, p. 4.

54 C. R. Peers (ed.), n.d. [1909], *The Book of the English Church Pageant, Fulham Palace June 10–16, 1909*, London: Eyre & Spottiswoode, pp. 2, 4–5.

55 Quoted in P. A. Rowe, 2011, 'The Roles of the Cathedral in the Modern English Church', unpublished PhD thesis, University of St Andrews, p. 39.

56 E. B. Pusey, 1833, *Remarks on the Prospective and Past Benefits of Cathedral Institutions*, London.

57 Chadwick, *Victorian Church*, Vol. 1, p. 140.

58 See Lord Henley, 1832, *A Plan of Church Reform*, London: Roake and Varty; and O. J. Brose, 1959, *Church & Parliament: The Reshaping of the Church of England, 1828–1860*, London: Oxford University Press.

59 P. Barrett, 1993, *Barchester: English Cathedral Life in the 19th century*, London: SPCK.

60 Barrett, *Barchester*, pp. 124, 141; see also P. J. Cadle, 'A new broom in the Augean Stable: Robert Gregory and Liturgical Changes at St Paul's Cathedral, London, 1868–1890', in R. N. Swanson (ed.), 1999, *Studies in Church History*, Vol. 35, Woodbridge: Boydell Press, pp. 361–73.

61 E. M. Goulburn, 1870, *The Principles of the Cathedral System*, London: Rivingtons.

62 Goulburn, *Principles*, pp. xiff.

63 E. W. Benson, 1871, 'Cathedral Life and Cathedral Work', *Quarterly Review*, vol. cxxx, no. 259; E. W. Benson, 1878, *The Cathedral: Its Necessary Place in the Life and work of the Church*, London.

64 G. W. Kitchin, 1895, *Edward Harold Browne, DD*, London: John Murray, p. 355.

65 In J. S Howson (ed.), 1872, *Essays on Cathedrals by various writers*, London: John Murray, p. 92.

66 J. J. Jusserand, 1889, *English Wayfaring Life in the Middle Ages*, London: Unwin; J. Cartwright, 1893, *The Pilgrims' Way from Winchester to Canterbury*, London: Virtue.

67 S. E. Lehmberg, 2005, *English Cathedrals: A History*, London and New York: Hambledon and London, p. 286.

68 O. Chadwick, 1977, 'From 1822 to 1916', in G. E. Aylmer and R. Cant (eds), *A History of York Minster*, Oxford: Clarendon Press, p. 272.

69 C. W. Stubbs, 1900, 'All saints and benefactors', in *Pro Patria: Sermons on special occasions in England and America*, London: Elliot Stock.

70 J. A. Stothert, 1843, *Justorum Semita; or, the Path of the Just. A History of the Saints and Holydays of the Present English Kalendar*, Edinburgh: R. Grant & Son, Aberdeen: A. Brown, London: James Burns, p. xvii.

71 Stothert, *Justorum Semita*, p. xxii.

72 G. H. Curteis, 1860, 'Cathedral restoration', in *Two sermons, preached in Lichfield Cathedral on February 5th and October 21st, 1860*, Oxford and London: J. H. & James Parker.

73 A. B. Clifton, 1898, *The cathedral church of Lichfield, a description of its fabric and a brief history of the Episcopal see*, London: George Bell & Sons, pp. 47–112; Anon., 1891, *Hand guide to Lichfield Cathedral, containing a detailed account of the sculpture on the west front and of the entire building and its contents, both inside and outside*, Lichfield: A. C. Lomax, p. 17.

74 H. E. Savage, n.d. [1914], *The Church heritage of Lichfield: an address given on the feast of St Chad, 1914*, Lichfield: A. C. Lomax, pp. 2–9.

75 For example, the first of the St Chad's lectures, given in 1913 by Dean Savage, with the title 'The Influence of St Chad', Lichfield: A. C. Lomax.

76 Greenslade, *Saint Chad*, p. 22.

77 Greenslade, *Saint Chad*, pp. 22–3.

78 P. Meadows and N. Ramsay (eds), 2003, *A History of Ely Cathedral*, Woodbridge: Boydell Press, p. 172.

79 Meadows and Ramsay, *Ely Cathedral*, p. 204 and footnote.

80 J. Bentham, 1771, *The History and Antiquities of the Conventual and Cathedral Church of Ely, From the Foundation of the Monastery, A.D. 673 to the year 1771*, Cambridge: Cambridge University Press, p. 285.

81 C. Merivale, n.d. [1873], *St. Etheldreda's Festival: Summary of proceedings with sermons and addresses at the bi-sexcentenary festival of St Etheldreda at Ely, October 1873*, London: Simpkin, Marshall, p. 23.

82 Baring-Gould, *Lives*, pp. 442–3.

83 See E. Roberts, 1993, *The Hill of the Martyr*, Dunstable: Book Castle, p. 103.

5

The twentieth century –
the renaissance gathers pace

By the end of the nineteenth century, cathedrals had begun to understand their vocation as places of welcome and pilgrimage. This, in turn, led to a greater understanding of the place of their own, indigenous saints and the role they might play in this process. But it was a progression not without its traumas ...

Opening up of cathedrals – places of welcome and pilgrimage

As the twentieth century dawned, cathedrals became more and more places where, in time, the ministry of saints and shrines to a wider constituency might once again find an honoured place. The century started well.

In 1917, Theodore Woods, bishop of Peterborough, initiated the practice of going on a pilgrimage through his diocese – a trend continued by Archbishop Garbett both at Winchester and York.[1]

This enthusiasm for pilgrimage became increasingly associated with cathedrals. Archbishop Benson, in his ministry at Truro, may have made cathedrals 'useful' but he failed to make them lovable. This became the task of Frank Bennett, dean of Chester. It was Dean Bennett who stressed that the cathedral should not only be a focus for the diocese but also a pilgrimage centre. In 1925, five years after he became dean of Chester, he published two books.[2] In these he encouraged the notion that the cathedral should be regarded as 'a home by the whole diocese, that in it every pilgrim from near or far may find Him, whose house it is'.[3] Bennett was convinced that a distinction must be drawn between visitors who are simply sightseers and 'pilgrims who come to listen and to talk to God'.[4] To encourage the latter he persuaded the Chapter to abolish entrance fees – to be followed in quick succession by Bristol, Ely, Salisbury and Worcester. Next he restored the monks' refectory at Chester to its ancient use as an eating place. A further step was the reintroduction of pilgrimage tokens, and he had copies made from ones used in medieval times at the shrine of St Werburgh in Chester, preserved in the British Museum. According to Bennett: 'Reproductions of this sign can be obtained from the cathedral vergers (1s); they carry with them for the modern pilgrim the obligation of saying a prayer in the cathedral.'[5]

Bennett's understanding of the role of a cathedral led him to emphasize the devotional aspect of pilgrimage:

> The primary business is to help those who come to feel and to profit by the religious impress of the place ... The heritage from the past should be made alive with religion for the needs and appreciation of today ... Every historic monument can be made alive with present day religious suggestion.[6]

Welcome and hospitality should be at the heart of every cathedral – 'open and free' were Bennett's watchwords. Those responsible should concentrate on 'making the whole place alive and religiously interesting, and especially interesting to the sort of people who travel by charabanc, as well as to the sort of people who travel by Rolls Royce'.[7]

Bennett's lead was followed by other cathedrals. In 1926, George Bell, two years after becoming dean of Canterbury, inspired a great diocesan pilgrimage to the cathedral. In 1927, the thirteen-hundredth anniversary of the founding of York Minster, there were 95 separate parish pilgrimages, with Cosmo Gordon Lang, as archbishop, presiding over the festivities.[8] In 1934, perhaps as a consequence of the Depression, some social workers advanced the idea of mass pilgrimages to all cathedrals – an idea taken up by many cathedrals, as a means of showing the nation's and the Church's concern for the unemployed. Between 1 and 14 July, great numbers attended, including the king and queen who went to Westminster Abbey and wore pilgrim badges. Everyone was asked to go to at least one cathedral during the fortnight and to make some offering, however small, which would be used for the unemployed.

Welcome and hospitality soon became part of the 'official' vocabulary of cathedrals. In 1924, the National Assembly of the Church of England set up a commission to consider the roles of cathedrals. One of the members was Dean Bennett. The commission's 1927 report summarized the cathedral's role as follows:

A cathedral, as the place of the bishop's seat, is the mother church of the diocese. To it, as the centre of their diocesan life, the clergy and the people will be encouraged to come; within it they will be made welcome; from it will go out into the diocese many activities helpful to the religious life of the people. The cathedral is a home and school of religious art – architecture, craftsmanship, and music – and religious learning.[9]

This opening up of cathedrals to wider constituencies continued with the formation of groups of Friends – groups of people, not necessarily worshippers, who wished the cathedral well and supported it financially. Starting with Dean George Bell's formation of the Friends of Canterbury Cathedral in 1927, many cathedrals followed suit during the 1930s.

At the same time, attitudes towards the saints and the departed began to develop. Chaplains returned from the Great War, demanding that there be some liturgical provision to help the bereaved hold onto hope in the face of such catastrophic numbers of dead. The Book of Common Prayer made very little such provision, and one of the key elements in the 1928 Prayer Book was that now there should be a 'Commemoration of All Souls'. The calendar of 1928 set out to provide the Church of England with a more representative group of saints to honour, not limited to the categories of apostle, evangelist and martyr.

In one sense, the Church of England was limited by its failure to have any official method of canonization, but it was realized that other means were possible. Thus, when the diocese of Lincoln wished to celebrate the fiftieth anniversary of the consecration of Bishop Edward King in 1935, it did so by making liturgical provision. A later report describes this:

> The Archbishop of Canterbury (Lang) celebrated a Solemn Eucharist in Lincoln Cathedral, at which, before a large and impressive congregation, the collect, epistle and gospel were proper to Edward King. This is a direct 'raising to the altar', an overt case of 'canonization' technically as may be. Whether the archbishop understood his own act is uncertain but probable; the bishop of Lincoln (Nugent Hicks) realized it clearly, prepared it deliberately, and forthwith issued the propers for use in the diocese on March 8 at the will of incumbents.[10]

Restoration – can a medieval shrine be reinvented? Two failed attempts and one success

The developments described above suggest that barriers were being broken down. Saints were now more acceptable in Anglican worship – cathedrals were becoming places of pilgrimage and welcome once again. Could it be that the time was right for the shrines of the saints to be revived and given back a creative use in cathedral life and liturgy?

Experiments in the late 1920s and 1930s proved far from propitious and showed that the Church of England was not quite ready.

The Tooth saga at Canterbury Cathedral, 1929–31

The shrines discussed so far have divided neatly along Anglican/Roman Catholic lines – the former taking 'remembrance' as their starting point, the latter placing great emphasis on the physical presence of saints' remains. Neither tradition saw their approach as any kind of restoration of pre-Reformation practice. Anglican cathedrals were naturally cautious about introducing anything that might suggest disloyalty to the Reformation, with its ambivalent views of the efficacy of saints and their prayers. Roman Catholic shrines, too, did not set out to recreate pre-Reformation circumstances – the Catholic Church clearly did not possess the buildings in which the shrines had been placed. The Roman Catholicism that returned with Emancipation in 1829 and the Restoration of the Hierarchy in 1850 was increasingly dependent not on the Catholicism that had existed before the Reformation but on a Catholicism influenced more by the Council of Trent and with the ultra-montanism of continental Catholicism.

However, one group in the Church of England had higher and different aspirations for at least one cathedral shrine – that of St Thomas Becket at Canterbury. The story of what took place during the years 1929–31, of the proposed restoration of pre-Reformation splendour, the heated discussions around the subject and its eventual failure, throws valuable light on how far the Church of England had yet to go in fully embracing the concept of a 'working' shrine. This was not achieved until 70 years later, at the very end of the twentieth century, and shows how conservative the Church of England still was in its attitudes to the saints.

The magnificent medieval shrine of St Thomas Becket is very well documented. It was the premier shrine of England, drawing pilgrims from across the western world, and the inspiration it gave to art, stained glass, music and literature was second to none.[11] The shrine became a symbol of church opposition to the crown, and its total destruction in 1538 took on major importance for Henry VIII and the emerging Protestant culture.[12]

After the Reformation, while some cathedrals preserved remnants of their shrines, Becket's former magnificence had to be divined from the stained-glass windows surrounding the Trinity Chapel in Canterbury Cathedral and from contemporary accounts. All that remained was the magnificently patterned floor on which the shrine had been placed and the ascending steps nearby, their treads hollowed by countless steps of pilgrims.[13] Unlike in St Albans and Chester, where modest restorations had been carried out, there certainly seemed little appetite on the part of the cathedral authorities in Canterbury to do anything about Becket's shrine.

The cause was taken up by the most extreme Anglo-Catholic wing of the Church of England, by the 1920s now in the ascendancy. Encouraged and emboldened by huge congresses in the Royal Albert Hall, Anglo-Catholics sensed, for the first time, real possibilities of reunion with Rome and did all in their power to present the Church of England as if the Reformation had not taken place. The Society of St Peter and St Paul, with its 'Back to Baroque' policies, now aimed to transform the externals of Anglican worship into the closest possible resemblance of continental Catholicism of the seventeenth and eighteenth centuries.[14] Devotions not envisaged by the most extreme adherents of the Oxford Movement – Benediction and Exposition of the Sacrament – were now encouraged, although fiercely denounced by most of the bench of bishops.

All this came at a time when there was great sensitivity to the return of elaborate ceremonial to the Church of England, with the rejection of the revised Prayer Book in 1928, partly on its perceived Anglo-Catholic stance. Thus, the atmosphere in English cathedrals – champions of the *via media* in Anglicanism – was far from receptive to anything of this sort and it is perhaps not surprising that the extreme proposals for a restoration of Becket's shrine were to fall on stony ground.

The 1929–31 scheme was the brainchild of Father Arthur Tooth. He had, famously, been caught up in the persecutions surrounding the 1874 Public Worship Regulation Act,[15] brought in for the purpose of putting down increasing ritualism. Fr Tooth, vicar of St James, Hatcham, was reported under the terms of the Act for using incense, vestments and candles.[16] When he refused to discontinue the use of

'The Christian Martyr'
Fr Arthur Tooth

these, he was briefly imprisoned and became, overnight, a martyr for the Anglo-Catholic cause.

After the fiasco of 1878, due to a breakdown in health, Tooth took on no further parochial responsibilities, but he used his considerable resources in founding an orphanage and a community of sisters. He purchased a mansion near Otford in Kent. It is on high ground overlooking part of the old Pilgrims' Way to Canterbury and so was of special interest to Fr Tooth, as he was devoted to St Thomas. This devotion reached a peak in 1929, when he proposed that a suitable shrine and memorial with an altar should be erected in Canterbury Cathedral, in keeping with the style of the twelfth century. He offered to put up an immediate £10,000 for the project, with a promise of obtaining a further £8,000, with £2,000 to be placed in the hands of trustees for upkeep of the restored shrine. The idea was warmly taken up by Viscount Halifax, doyen of the Anglo-Catholic wing of the Church, President of the English Church Union and champion of Anglican/Roman-Catholic reunion,[17] and it was Lord Halifax who first seems to have proposed the matter to colleagues. In a letter to Fr F. G. Croom, vicar of St Cuthbert, Philbeach Gardens in London, he wrote enthusiastically:

> One feels it is an act of Justice in regard to the way St Thomas was treated by Henry II and Henry VIII, and surely over and above such considerations Thomas a Becket's own merits and history are surely worthy of such a recognition on the part of those who desire to vindicate the rights of the Church and enable it to bear that witness ...[18]

Indeed, Lord Halifax, from the start, saw this restoration as having positive reverberations far beyond the confines of Canterbury:

> Was there ever a moment in the history of the world when it was more apparent that the only true and possible solution of all our political,

social and religious difficulties is to be found in the honest and true vindication of Christian Principles?[19]

The matter had been passed before the previous dean of Canterbury, George Bell, who was now bishop of Chichester, and from Chichester, when consulted, he raised grave concerns:

> On the one hand one cannot but be aware of the need of a better furnishing of the High Altar and the whole sanctuary and of the vacant space east of the High Altar in the Trinity Chapel itself. It must strike many religious observers that there is a bareness in the very place which in former ages was a great centre of devotion ...[20]

Bell, however, in the same memorandum, warned that 'fears and suspicions' might arise because of the scheme:

> It might be interpreted as provocative on the ecclesiastical side, viz. Church and State. It might also be interpreted as the flying of a turbulent Anglo-Catholic flag and another sign of a great move forward in that direction. It can hardly be denied that the moment for inviting such a controversy is inopportune, in view of the Prayer Book controversy immediately behind us and about us, and also in view of the Lambeth Conference next year. It would be most undesirable that Canterbury Cathedral should be the storm centre of an ecclesiastical controversy.

Bishop Bell warned that the archbishop of Canterbury, Cosmo Lang, should be consulted, as it raised key questions for the Church of England. Was it a shrine or a memorial that was to be restored? Could this be genuine, as there was no actual tomb now present? What did this say about the nature of Anglican ecclesiology? Bell himself preferred something much more modest: a scheme in which the Chapter would take control rather than be beholden to outside and extreme influences – and that Chapter should choose their own architect.

The Chapter of Canterbury warmed to Bell's concerns and addressed the proposal in a Chapter meeting in February 1930. They clearly preferred the term 'memorial' rather than Tooth's 'altar shrine', as the latter suggested that the relics of the martyr would be enclosed *in* the shrine, which was clearly impossible, and also the revival of medieval pilgrimage, which was felt to be undesirable. They therefore put forward their own, more modest proposals, consisting of a 'memorial cenotaph' with an altar 'of exquisite workmanship', venturing the hope that the donor 'may be willing to accept such suggestions as sufficiently fulfilling the laudable intentions of all concerned'.[21]

The Chapter's reflections were confirmed by Archbishop Lang,[22] and the decision of the Chapter communicated to the donor.[23] At the same time, these ecclesiastical and aesthetic reservations were supplemented by concerns about the cost of the project:

> the individual members of the Chapter were many of them very gravely disturbed in mind at the idea of the expenditure of anything like so large a sum as £20,000 or even £10,000 for such a purpose, even as a gift, at a time when money was so badly needed for work overseas, for Church extension at home ...[24]

Lord Halifax was singularly unimpressed with what he construed as weak-minded indecision:

> I can hardly say how horrible it seems to me and how distressing, even the thought that so splendid a proposal, and one involving such magnificent possibilities should even be *thought* to be in danger of coming to naught, and being set aside as a failure.[25]

In the same letter, he proposed that, at his own expense, designs should be produced by the eminent architect Sir Ninian Comper,[26] again taking the opportunity to impress upon the Chapter the seemingly world-changing power that this project would have, if accepted:

> It is a matter that concerns not merely England and England's church but the whole Christian world, and, at this moment, by the striking contrast it would offer, teach the world at large the difference between the convictions and actions of Englishmen who fear God and have His honour and the respect due to His Saints at heart, and those who in what was once Christian Russia are doing all in their power to ruin God's Church in their unhappy country and destroy the faith of its children.

In July 1930, Comper revealed his plans for the shrine; clearly, none of the wishes of the Dean and Chapter had been followed or incorporated. When Comper met with the Chapter on 30 July, the plans showed an enormous structure, 16 feet high, 16 feet long and 12 feet wide – a structure that compromised the high altar of the cathedral and completely altered the character of the east end of the cathedral.[27]

*Sir Ninian Comper's design for the shrine of St Thomas
of Canterbury (1930) – 1*

The matter was not helped by Comper's receiving from Dean Sheppard
a letter, written from his sickbed, which appeared to be rather more
enthusiastic than members of his Chapter. The dean suggested that in
order to move the matter forward a full-size silhouette or mock-up be
commissioned and set up on the proposed site.[28]

Meanwhile, Lord Halifax's enthusiasm knew no bounds, and in a letter to the dean he referred to a conversation with the bishop of Truro,
in which the bishop had alluded to the likelihood of the discovery of
Becket's bones and therefore the possibility of there being relics in the
restored shrine – not a development that would have encouraged the
Chapter at all!

*Sir Ninian Comper's design for the shrine of
St Thomas of Canterbury (1930) – 2*

Only think what an opportunity there is before Chapter? The bones
could be placed within the shrine, and the monument would not only
be a monument to the memory of St Thomas but the actual place in
which, after all these years, his bones would actually rest. Is it not
something almost too glorious and splendid to think of? Could we ever
forgive ourselves if we let slip and missed so great an opportunity?[29]

Such pushing of the boundaries was causing the Chapter even greater
concern, and the archdeacon of Canterbury wrote with passion on the
matter:

I feared from the first that, having agreed to the general idea, we
might find ourselves being pushed much further than we wished to go.
This is exactly what has happened.[30]

The silhouette or mock-up of the shrine was erected in the cathedral on
29 September 1930 and various people invited to comment. Particularly
incisive was the Revd C. E. Woodruff, 'Six Preacher' of the cathedral,

Mock-up of Comper's design

who expressed the view that the scheme was 'too grandiose a character to be suitable in a church whose custodians have no desire to revive the cult of St Thomas'. He opined that modern tombs over the bodies of ancient saints possess little interest – he gave as an example the seventeenth-century shrine of St Edmund of Pontigny, and suggested that a cenotaph erected at Canterbury 760 years after the death of the man it commemorates would have even less relevance.

This last question linked with those being asked about the restoration of the shrine at Walsingham at this very time, in which 'traditions' were being presented with very little historical or physical evidence to substantiate them.

Comper himself was pleased with the result of the model and wrote to the dean about it:

May it not be said at Canterbury that the very existence of the east end where we propose to put this monument was due to St Thomas? ... My hope all through has been that the proposal might be saved from being a party matter as St Thomas, apart from all party questions, is indisputably not only one of England's great men, but the outstanding figure by which Canterbury Cathedral is known to the whole world. No one realizing this could think for a moment that what we propose would be to give him an undue prominence in the Cathedral ... all will agree that it is time that quiet and unostentatious, but adequate amends, such as we hope this is, were made.[31]

'Quiet and unostentatious' was certainly in the minds of the Chapter, but it is questionable how far Comper's enormous structure could possibly have fulfilled this!

The final blow came on 31 October 1930, when Chapter met to reject Comper's proposals, stressing that while they admired its artistic merits they were unable to proceed with the scheme – it was too dominant in the cathedral and it paid too much homage to Becket and placed other saints of Canterbury (Alphege, Augustine, Dunstan) in a lesser light:

> The Dean and Chapter cannot but think that this would place such emphasis on the historical significance of St Thomas as would affect the mind and feeling of the whole Anglican Communion towards Canterbury Cathedral in a way which many would regret.[32]

Lord Halifax, of course, was furious and threatened to come immediately to Canterbury to arraign the Chapter personally. He also, in desperation, suggested that the Comper scheme be transferred from its proposed position in the Trinity Chapel to a less obvious one on the site of Becket's martyrdom – a suggestion hardly less controversial and impractical.[33]

In the event, death put an end to the scheme. Fr Tooth died on 6 March 1931 at the age of 91, and his executors showed no willingness to extend the financial arrangement. Halifax continued for some time to criticize publicly the Chapter and to express his sorrow that the scheme had fallen:

> The offer about the monument to St Thomas and the shrine in your cathedral, owing to the death of the donor, has come to an end. I must say I am very sorry that such should be the fact and I also see what a misfortune it was that your late Dean was unable to do anything in the matter. Had the plan been realized it would have been very delightful in all ways as such a monument would have been appreciated as much abroad as it would have been in England.[34]

His parting shot deserves quotation:

> As to the Chapter of Canterbury, no words can say what I think about them. I don't see how any set of people could have behaved worse or in a more absolutely foolish way than they have. One could not have supposed that any set of reasonable men could have acted as they did.[35]

The Chapter, meanwhile, took stock of the situation and their attitude may be summarized in a letter from the archdeacon of Canterbury:

> When Mr. Comper was asked to prepare a design we understood that our answer was acceptable. But his design clearly showed that it was not understood by him. Until he does understand our mind, and produces something more in accordance with it, I do not think we shall get any further. Much as I would like to have a worthy memorial to St Thomas, I would rather have nothing at all than something which is not appreciated by us, and the majority of those whose feelings we must regard.[36]

And 'nothing at all' in the words of the archdeacon summarizes best what subsequently happened to the shrine area. In the spring of 1946, there was a suggestion that the 'Burial Site of St Thomas' in the crypt should be marked with a cross and the grave surrounded with posts and cords. A drawing was made in October 1946, but the Chapter postponed the matter, indicating that they would look at the tomb of the Unknown Warrior in Westminster Abbey as an example. The scheme was not pursued, but, in May 1948, Seeley and Paget, an architectural firm who were doing other work for the Chapter, were asked to advise about the best method of marking the burial place. Like Comper in 1930, the firm produced a grandiose scheme, quite unlike the Chapter's former suggestion. This was turned down as 'too elaborate' in April 1949. Eventually, in July 1949, the grave was reopened so that the bones could be studied by anatomy experts. They reported in 1951 that the bones were probably not those of St Thomas, so the scheme for marking the place was dropped.[37]

And so, in both cases, no major marking of these significant points in the cathedral was undertaken, and the site of Becket's shrine in the Trinity Chapel has, since the late 1970s, been marked with a simple inscription cut into the marble, with a single candle burning continually. In many ways, this utter simplicity provides perhaps the greatest effectiveness.

Shrine area at Canterbury Cathedral today

The saga of 1929–31, although it failed to produce a major restoration of the shrine of St Thomas, was highly significant in drawing out Anglican attitudes to this most controversial area. It showed that the Anglican method of 'remembrance' was, at least at that time, deemed much more inclusive and found greater and wider support. The matter showed that there was resistance in attempting to 'restore' a shrine when there was little or nothing on which to base that restoration. Subsequent restorations (St Albans, Hereford and Oxford) have been successful as the authorities were dealing with a substantial fragment on which to build (generally a shrine base). The Tooth saga showed, too, that cathedrals were not ready, at least not in the late 1920s, to throw in their lot with the Anglo-Catholic wing of the Church of England, and still held a very cautious view as to how saints' remains should be viewed and how prayers to the saints should be addressed. It needed a more open understanding of 'churchmanship' in the Church of England, together with major developments in perceiving the role of cathedrals, theologically and spiritually, and of pilgrimage, commerce and inclusiveness.

St Davids – Anglicans and Roman Catholics diverge in devotion to St David

So far, we have seen a major difference in ways in which Anglicans and Roman Catholics began to establish shrines of the saints in their churches and cathedrals. For Roman Catholics, the presence of relics in the shrine was all-important; for Anglicans, this was a step too far and 'remembrance' was felt to be the right approach.

In the case of St David, such approaches were reversed – it was the Anglicans who stressed the importance of the relics of this great saint of the Welsh, whereas the Roman Catholics contented themselves with much more modest claims.

We have seen the medieval context of St David's cult. The shrine of 1275, fitting centrally within the north choir arcade, had a southern 'show' elevation, richly decorated with icons, while a simpler north elevation faced into the choir aisle. This shrine survived the onslaught of the Reformation, when the newly appointed bishop, William Barlow, seized the relics when they were brought out for display on St David's day 1538. Antiquarians of the eighteenth century marvelled at this survival, and in Browne Willis's Survey of 1717 he states:

> On the north side of the chancel, near the Steeple, under an arch, is St David's Tomb. Formerly it was all of one flat stone, which is now broken into several pieces; above it, were anciently three images – St David's in the middle. St Patrick's on the right hand and St Dennis's on the left, as Tradition informs us.

New interest in the shrine was kindled as part of the major restoration of the cathedral under the direction of George Gilbert Scott in the 1860s. A major survey by W. B. Jones and E. A. Freeman provided detailed descriptions of the shrines of both St David and St Caradoc as regards their archaeological significance, but gave little information on the cultic use of each.[38]

However, when interest in St David emerged in the twentieth century, it was not this shrine that provided a focus of attention but the 'rediscovery' of bones declared by the then dean, William Williams, to be those of St David himself. There was no concrete evidence that they were – even circumstantial evidence was against the claim. However, to Williams, and arguably the fledgling Church in Wales, enthusiastic to secure its claim to continuity, they were a godsend. Dean Williams had the bones placed in an arched recess in the west wall of the Trinity

*Shrine with 'relics' of St David, Trinity Chapel,
St Davids Cathedral*

Chapel, behind the high altar, and the whole enclosed with an orna-mental iron screen, through which the reliquary could be seen and touched.

With the 'relics' of St David safely back in a place of honour in the cathedral, Dean Williams cemented the Church of Wales' claim to historic continuity with the age of the saints still further in July 1925, when he organized an ecumenical service to commemorate the sixteen-hundredth anniversary of the Council of Nicaea. The service was attended by Anglicans, Nonconformists and representatives of the Eastern Orthodox churches – but, significantly, Roman Catholics were not invited. In his sermon, the first archbishop of Wales, A. G. Edwards, made a point of insisting on the Church in Wales' continuity with the ancient churches of the East and not with the Latin West (David had been consecrated, by tradition, in Jerusalem). The service was interpreted by many as a snub against the Roman Catholics.

Dean Williams was also responsible for the revival of organized pilgrimages to the cathedral and now to the restored shrine. In this he was supported by Arthur Baring-Gould, the eccentric vicar of St Martin's Haverfordwest, from where pilgrims departed for their itinerary, which included a visit to the reliquary in the Trinity Chapel in the cathedral.[39]

At the same time, and partly spurred on by the less than ecumenical approach of the cathedral itself, Roman Catholics were developing their own tradition. On St David's day 1934, the foundation stone of a new chapel was laid by Bishop Francis Vaughan of Menevia. The chapel was dedicated to St Non, mother of St David – on the site generally believed to have been the birthplace of St David. The new chapel was consecrated a year later by Francis Mostyn, archbishop of Cardiff. St Non's Chapel would not house any relics of the saint, but rather a greater Presence – that of Christ in the Blessed Sacrament. In a sermon in August 1934, Archbishop Mostyn contrasted the new chapel, 'where the faithful can receive the Sacrament instituted by our Divine Saviour and listen to the Gospel and the teaching which he taught his disciples',[40] with the cathedral where, until the sixteenth century, 'the Holy Sacrifice of the Mass was offered up, and where the Blessed Sacrament of the Holy Eucharist was reserved', but not thereafter. 'Although used for the worship of God ... no longer the [home] of Jesus in the Sacrament of the Blessed Eucharist', was his verdict upon St Davids and the other Anglican cathedrals and churches in Wales.[41]

The restoration of various devotions to St David emerged amid dubious historic authenticity and regrettable denominational rivalry. It would be another 70 years before the shrine of St David in the cathedral itself was restored, in an atmosphere of greater ecumenical co-operation.

Walsingham – supreme example of a shrine restored

The original image of Our Lady of Walsingham was burnt by the Reformers in 1538, when the Walsingham shrine was suppressed. The devotion was never forgotten, however, and over the centuries an antiquarian interest persisted.[42] By the mid 1930s, two parallel shrines had been developed – Anglican and Roman Catholic – and both testified to the increasing popularity and power of shrines in the twentieth century.

The Roman Catholics focused their devotion on the Slipper Chapel in the village of Houghton St Giles, about a mile from the centre of Walsingham. The chapel is a fourteenth-century building, which was probably the last stopping point on the medieval pilgrim road to Walsingham before reaching the shrine. The chapel had been bought by a wealthy woman called Charlotte Boyd, who converted to Catholicism soon after the purchase. The first official pilgrimage to Walsingham took place on 20 August 1897. Although the chapel did not come into active use until the 1930s, it provided Roman Catholics with a genuinely medieval building and an important set of credentials as they established their place at Walsingham.[43]

Meanwhile, Anglican devotion was developing in parallel. In 1922, Alfred Hope Patten, vicar of St Mary's church, Little Walsingham, rededicated a replica of the medieval statue and set it up in the parish church. Regular devotions and pilgrimages became increasingly popular and, in conflict with the Anglican hierarchy and in particular with the bishop of Norwich, Patten decided to move his shrine and statue out of the parish church onto land privately owned by the Anglo-Catholic Society of Our Lady of Walsingham. There, on a site within yards of the ruins of the Augustinian priory, a new shrine church was built, designed and funded by Sir William Milner, with 15 chapels associated with the mysteries of the rosary and an inner chapel, or 'holy house', where the image of Our Lady of Walsingham was venerated.[44]

Translation of the image of Our Lady of Walsingham to the new shrine (15 October 1932)

Patten and his supporters saw themselves as reviving the lost medieval Catholic tradition in England, which they did not see as synonymous with the Church of Rome. Indeed, when on 15 October 1932 Patten led a procession of 3,000 pilgrims which translated the image to the new shrine, he proclaimed that the Holy House was:

> as far as we know, the first Chapel built by English Catholics from all over the country, since the Dissolution, for the express purpose of raising a Sanctuary for the housing of a Shrine, in the real sense of the word. In ancient days, it was the foremost holy place in England; the National Shrine. It is fitting in the steady course of Catholic revival in this land, that it should be the first re-erected.[45]

Reactions to the revived shrine were numerous and often outraged. In the *Evening Standard* on 1 September 1926, Hensley Henson, bishop of Durham, wrote a furious attack:

> The attempt to revive pilgrimages can only succeed if it carries the religious Englishman back to the spiritual level of the Middle Ages ... the revived pilgrimages ... are rather 'pageants' than religious acts. The pitiable rubbish of the Walsingham processional hymn could only be intelligible as part of a 'pageant'. As an act of religion, it would be profane.[46]

Further developments included Patten's claim to have discovered the original holy well and incorporated this into the shrine church; and, in order to authenticate continuity with the medieval church, he made a large collection of stones gathered from monasteries and other religious houses dissolved by Henry VIII. These he incorporated into the exterior faces of the Holy House and into the high altar of the shrine church:

> The altar [inside the Holy House] is built of stones, chiefly from the ruined priory of our Lady of Walsingham, but among others from Binham Abbey, a cell of the great Benedictine Abbey of St Albans, the Pilgrim Chapel of Our Lady of the Red Mount at Lynn, Rievaulx Abbey, the first Cistercian house in Yorkshire, colonized directly from St Bernard's own Clairvaux, Dunwich Priory, near the site of the submerged East Anglian Cathedral, Netley Abbey, Barking Abbey, founded by St Erkenwald for his sister St Ethelburga, another Cistercian monastery colonized from Savigny and Furnes and Mileham Priory.[47]

In Walsingham, we have an example of a shrine that succeeded in reviving and reinventing its medieval past. Whereas Canterbury Cathedral felt unable to embrace a major change in thinking, which might have seemed disloyal to the Reformation, the authorities at Walsingham had no such scruples – indeed, Patten had a great deal more freedom than had any cathedral Chapter, bounded as they were by statute and episcopal watchfulness.[48] What is more, the devotion at Walsingham re-established during the 1920s was sustained and became a major part of the spirituality of the Catholic tradition of the Church of England, as we shall see in a later chapter.

Roman Catholics raise the profile of the shrine

Part of the reticence of Anglicans for 'going all the way' with restorations of saints' shrines was a continuing fear and suspicion of Roman Catholic practices. This is undoubtedly what was in the mind of Canterbury's authorities when they set their face against any major restoration of Becket's cult. When we see what was happening at Westminster Cathedral at about the same time, we begin to understand their reservations.

Westminster Cathedral – St John Southworth and Catholic triumphalism

> ... a witness of special importance in these days when there is a tendency to gloss over the essential difference between Catholic and Protestant. When John Southworth lived and toiled and died, the difference was clearly known and fully acknowledged. In the case of every one of our Martyrs it is evident that, had they been willing to call themselves Protestants and give up the name of Catholic, to abjure the Mass and accept the Protestant 'Communion Service', none would have been brought to trial for treason, or put to death as a traitor. The issue was a purely religious one, and the charge of treason a miserable subterfuge, devoid of proof of any kind, whereby Englishmen, than whom none were ever more loyal to their country, were doomed to death because they were determined to give God the things that are God's whilst they gave all allegiance to Caesar in the things that are truly Caesar's.[49]

Cardinal Bourne's introduction to the only major biography of St John Southworth immediately gets to the heart of the meaning of this, the premier shrine in any Catholic cathedral in England. If St Chad's shrine in the cathedral in Birmingham used Chad's Saxon relics to authenticate the continuity of the Catholic Church before and after the Reformation – and indeed, of an age before the era of canonization – the great crystal reliquary, containing the complete embalmed body of this Catholic priest who was hanged, drawn and quartered for his Catholic faith in the mid-seventeenth century, in Westminster Cathedral speaks powerfully of a church honed by cruel martyrdom and now proudly proclaiming its authenticity, in complete contrast to the state Protestant Church, as it was seen.

John Southworth was born in Lancashire in 1592. Ordained as a priest at the English College in Douai, he returned to England in 1619 and ministered to the people of his native Lancashire until his arrest in 1627. After spending three years in prison, he was delivered along with 15 other priests into the hands of the French ambassador for transportation abroad. Returning secretly to England, he was again arrested and imprisoned. Released in 1636, he took up residence in London and ministered to those dying of the plague, winning many deathbed converts. He was arrested again in 1637. After spending a further three years in prison, he was again liberated in July 1640 and continued to minister. His final arrest led to his trial at which, against the advice of his counsel, he insisted on pleading 'guilty' to being a priest and was consequently condemned to death. At the age of 62 he was hanged, drawn and quartered at Tyburn on 18 July 1654.[50]

Southworth's body was handed into the custody of the family of the Duke of Norfolk, who had it embalmed and sent to the English College at Douai. The body was sewn together, buried and venerated as a relic until the French Revolution, when it was hidden in an unmarked grave to save it from destruction by the secular fundamentalist Revolutionaries. The grave was rediscovered in 1927 and Southworth's remains were returned to England.

On 1 May 1930 the body was enshrined in a crystal casket and solemnly placed in the Chapel of St George and the English martyrs in Westminster Cathedral. Southworth was beatified by Pope Pius XI in 1929 and canonized by Pope Paul VI in 1970.

Immediately, the new shrine was seen as a potential draw for pilgrims:

> it is quite in order that the large shrine of Blessed John Southworth, containing the almost complete body of that heroic stalwart, should have place there, as we are confident that it will become a much visited goal for pilgrims.[51]

Descriptions of the elaborate translation of Southworth's body on 1 May conclude with similar aspirations for the new shrine:

> Continuous streams of pilgrims visited the shrine and resting place of one whom His Eminence hopes will henceforth be the patron and model for the secular clergy of the Westminster Archdiocese.[52]

Shrine of St John Southworth, Westminster Cathedral

Sermons preached on the days leading up to the translation of the body emphasized the courage of Southworth as an example for clergy, living in more emancipated times, while Fr John H. Filmer, Master of the Guild of Our Lady of Ransom, was unequivocal in his view of the new shrine:

> In Westminster Abbey was the tomb of an unknown warrior, typical of those who died to save England in the Great War. In Westminster Cathedral there was now the body of a known warrior, who had died to save England in the Great War against the Church of Christ.[53]

The shrine was inaugurated shortly after the centenary of Catholic Emancipation in 1929, so it was understandable that this shrine, with its overtones of anti-Protestant sentiment, should be viewed as a powerful symbol of how far the Catholic Church had progressed in those hundred years.

> In his dying speech at Tyburn, he pleaded for 'the poor distressed Catholics I leave behind me'; and we who have lived to see the centenary of our Emancipation must always remember with deep thankfulness that the men who made possible our Catholic England

of today were Englishmen of the stamp of Blessed John Southworth, priest and martyr.[54]

But there is more. The setting up of this shrine came at a time when the Catholic Church was refocusing its mission in a triumphalist way. This was the era of the setting up of the feast of Christ the King in 1925. The papacy, betrayed by the old European powers when it lost the papal states, now took a much wider view of Catholic fortunes than simply the devastation in Europe – Christ the King, or at least his Vicar on earth, had the task of integrating all society under a single monarchy.[55] Foreign missions, so often the preserve of Protestant mission societies in the nineteenth century, now looked to Rome for inspiration, and the Irish Catholic Church, previously remarkably inward-looking, was beginning to produce great numbers of clergy and nuns for mission abroad. Benedict XV's apostolic letter of 1919, *Maximum Illud*, heralded an age in which the Roman Catholic Church had become the largest single component in the Christian world family of churches. The use of a saint's relics to create popular fervour to underline the power-ful role of the Church in post-war Europe is seen in high profile in the canonization of St Thérèse of Lisieux and in the building of a great basilica to contain her shrine. France's humiliation in the Great War was addressed positively by the papacy and the new shrine provided an ideal focus for this.[56] In England, Cardinal Francis Bourne held sway over a Roman Catholic Church enjoying ever greater popularity in the land, and marked by an increasing conservatism – new schools and churches were being built and the Catholic Church found influence in the highest levels of society. The finding in 1927 of the relics of such a high-profile saint as John Southworth seemed God-given, and the triumphal translation of his embalmed remains to their new shrine in the premier Catholic church of the realm chimed with so much that was happening in the worldwide Catholic Church, and seemed to symbolize the ascendancy of the Roman Catholic Church in Britain.[57]

Notes

1 C. Smyth, 1959, *Cyril Forster Garbett, Archbishop of York*, London: Hodder & Stoughton, pp. 150, 216, 272f.

2 F. Bennett, 1925, *Chester Cathedral*, Chester: Phillipson & Golder; F. Bennett, 1925, *The Nature of a Cathedral*, Chester: Phillipson & Golder.

3 Bennett, *Nature*, pp. 467f.

4 Bennett, *Nature*, p. 5.

5 Bennett, *Nature*, p. 89.

6 Bennett, *Nature*, pp. 48–52.

7 Bennett, *Nature*, p. 46.

8 J. S. Lockhart, 1949, *Cosmo Gordon Lang*, London: Hodder & Stoughton, pp. 296f.

9 *Report of the Cathedrals Commission Appointed in Pursuance of a Resolution of the National Assembly of the Church of England*, 1927, London: Church Assembly and SPCK, pp. 9–10.

10 *The Commemoration of Saints and Heroes in the Anglican Communion*, 1957, pp. 31f.

11 See D. Stevens, 1970, *Music in Honour of St Thomas of Canterbury*, London: Novello.

12 P. Collinson, N. Ramsay and M. Sparks, 1995, A *History of Canterbury Cathedral*, Oxford: Oxford University Press, pp. 154–5.

13 Collinson et al., *History*, p. 155.

14 See P. F. Anson, 1960, *Fashions in Church Furnishings, 1840–1940*, London: Faith Press, pp. 316–17.

15 See O. Chadwick, 1966/1971, *The Victorian Church*, London: Adam and Charles Black, Vol. 2, pp. 322–5.

16 J. Coombs, 1969, *Judgement on Hatcham: The History of a Religious Struggle, 1877–1886*, London: Faith Press; *Project Canterbury, Arthur Tooth*, 1933, London: The Catholic Literature Association.

17 J. G. Lockhart, 1935–36, *Charles Lindley, Viscount Halifax*, London: G. Bles.

18 Tooth Correspondence (hereafter *Tooth*), ADD MS 366/2, Halifax to Revd F. G. Croom, 26 May 1929.

19 *Tooth*, 366/2.

20 *Tooth*, Memorandum from George Bell, bishop of Chichester, 6 August 1929.

21 Canterbury Cathedral, Chapter Act Book, 1924–31, 14 and 22 February, 1930. CAA – DCC – CA/18, 787 and 789 (hereafter CAA).

22 Memo of interview given by the archbishop to the archdeacon of Canterbury and Canon Jenkins, 16 February 1930, *Tooth*, 366/2.

23 CAA, 789.

24 Memo by Dr Jenkins at an interview with Mr Croom and Prebendary Mackay, 7 April 1930. *Tooth*, 366/1,

25 Letter, Halifax to Croom, *Tooth*, 366/2, 5 May 1930.

26 A. Symondson and S. Bucknall, 2006, *Sir Ninian Comper: An Introduction to His Life and Work with Complete Gazeteer*, London: Spire Books.

27 *Tooth*, 366/1, 30 July 1930.

28 Letter, dean of Canterbury to Comper, *Tooth*, 366/1, 1 August 1930.

29 Letter, Halifax to dean of Canterbury, *Tooth*, 366/1, 15 August 1930.

30 Memo, archdeacon of Canterbury, *Tooth*, 366/1, 18 August 1930.

31 Letter, Comper to dean of Canterbury, *Tooth*, 366/1, 8 October 1930.

32 CAA, 937.

33 Letter, Halifax to Comper, *Tooth*, 366/1, 5 November 1930.

34 Letter, Halifax to Bickersteth, *Tooth*, 366/2, 1 April 1931.

35 Letter, Halifax to Croom, *Tooth*, 366/2, 27 July 1931.

36 Letter, archdeacon of Canterbury to Croom, *Tooth*, 366/1, 27 February 1931.

37 Note supplied to me by Cressida Williams, archivist, Canterbury Cathedral.

38 W. B. Jones and E. A. Freeman, 1856, *The History and Antiquities of St. David's*. See 1998 edition, Pembrokeshire County Council Cultural Services, pp. 102–7.

39 See J. Morgan-Guy, 2007, 'Shrine and counter-shrine in 1920s and 1930s Dewisland?', in J. Wyn Evans and J. M. Wooding (eds), *St David of Wales: Cult, Church and Nation*, Woodbridge: Boydell Press, pp. 286–95.

40 C. H. Morgan-Griffiths, 1934, *Chapel of Our Lady and St Non*, privately printed, p. 21.

41 Morgan-Griffiths, *Chapel*, pp. 20–1. This was a favourite theme of Mostyn's. Five years before he had claimed that the cathedrals 'stood as cold and empty shells awaiting the time when new life would be infused into them, and they would once more be used for the purpose for which they were erected', *Western Mail*, 15 October 1929, quoted by T. O. Hughes, 2001, 'Continuity and conversion: the concept of a national church in twentieth-century Wales and its relation to the Celtic Church', in R. Pope (ed.), *Religion and National Identity, Wales and Scotland c.1700–2000*, Cardiff: University of Wales Press, p. 131.

42 See J. C. Dickenson, 1956, *The Shrine of Our Lady of Walsingham*, Cambridge: Cambridge University Press.

43 See S. Coleman and J. Elsner, 1999, 'Pilgrimage to Walsingham and the Re-Invention of the Middle Ages', in J. Stopford, *Pilgrimage Explored,* York: York Medieval Press, pp. 189ff.

44 M. Yelton, 2006, *Alfred Hope Patten and the Shrine of Our Lady of Walsingham*, Norwich: Canterbury Press.

45 *Our Lady's Mirror*, Autumn 1931, p. 1.

46 See also O. Chadwick, 1983, *Hensley Henson: A Study in the Friction between Church and State*, Oxford: Clarendon Press.

47 *Our Lady's Mirror*, Winter, 1932, p. 3.

48 See C. Stephenson, 1970, *Walsingham Way*, London: Faith Press, 1970.

49 A. B. Purdie, 1930, *The Life of Blessed John Southworth*, London: Burns, Oates & Washbourne, pp. xiii–xiv.

50 See 'Blessed John Southworth and his time', *The Month*, Jan–Jun 1930, pp. 351–4.

51 *The Tablet*, Vol. CLV (10 April, 1930), p. 511.

52 *The Tablet*, p. 511.

53 *The Tablet*, p. 511.

54 Purdie, *Life*, p. 175.

55 D. MacCulloch, 2009, *A History of Christianity*, London: Allen Lane, p. 931.

56 See 'Celine Martin's images of Thérèse of Lisieux and the creation of a modern saint', in P. Clark and T. Claydon (eds), 2011, *Saints and Sanctity*, Studies in Church History, Vol. 47, Woodbridge: Boydell and Brewer.

57 E. Norman, 1985, *Roman Catholicism in England from the Elizabethan Settlement to the Second Vatican Council*, Oxford: Oxford University Press, pp. 110–11.

6

The story continues –
the shrines of the saints return

By the mid-twentieth century, the atmosphere was changing. Cathedrals were developing their roles in mission and worship and were, once again, becoming places receptive to a wide range of devotional practices – practices that would at one time have been considered highly disloyal to the Reformation.

Cathedrals discover new roles

During the second half of the twentieth century, cathedrals began to find a new role. The 1963 Cathedrals Measure set out guidelines for revision of cathedral statutes; however, it was not to be legislation that would change the face of cathedral ministry but rather a response to circumstances and changes in Church and society. The new cathedral at Coventry, built in the 1950s, held up a vision of what a cathedral might be. The provost of the time, Howard William, propounded new uses of his cathedral, with experimental work in:

- Liturgy and worship.
- Industrial relations.
- Commerce.
- Social services.
- Music in the cathedral and the community.
- International Christian contacts.
- Youth activities, local, national and international.
- The use of drama as a means of communication.
- Education (schools and colleges).
- Adult education.
- Ecumenical enterprises.
- The pastoral needs of the congregation.

- The ministry to visitors and pilgrims.
- The administration of the cathedral.[1]

Tourism grew in the years following the 1960s, as did the giving of greater priority by the state to the preservation of cultural treasures. In 1979 the English Tourist Board published *English Cathedrals and Tourism*,[2] which sought to show how people could be helped to enjoy the experience of visiting cathedrals and illustrated ways in which revenue might be increased to support these expensive buildings. Other studies followed, not least Myra Shackley's *Managing Sacred Sites*.[3] In this, tourism and theology were brought close together; she describes what motivates visitors to sacred sites:

> [They] are seeking an experience to change them, but not all are seeking that experience for the same reasons. The managers of sacred sites have to cater for this need while avoiding bringing the attendee down to earth. The experience should be essentially spiritual, uncontaminated by technical and commercial realities. Sacred sites should offer the attendee a window on infinity. As Albert Einstein famously said, 'The fairest thing that we can experience is the mysterious'. It is the task of sacred sites to manage the mysterious and reach for the sublime while coping with the prosaic. Whatever the shape of the post-modern world, increasing numbers of people are going to be looking at sacred sites for some means of defining a more acceptable reality.[4]

Cathedrals responded to this new spirit in many ways. Durham Cathedral was one of the first to set up a professional restaurant in its precincts (1977), and by the end of the twentieth century there was hardly a cathedral without its shop and cafe/restaurant. Cathedrals with monastic histories saw this as the continuation of a Benedictine tradition of hospitality, but all realized the potential of a warm welcome in enabling visitors and pilgrims to experience the heart of the cathedral.

Yet this approach was not without its dangers, and various controversies during the 1980s, not least at Hereford over the Mappa Mundi and at Lincoln over commercial and relational concerns, led to the publication of the 1994 report *Heritage and Renewal*.[5] This sought to 'examine the future role in Church and nation of the Cathedrals of the Church of England, and to make recommendations as to how best that role could be fulfilled, including proposals for their government and support'.[6]

The tension between religion and commerce had, arguably, been present in medieval cathedrals, where custodians of shrines sought to use their spiritual resources to generate income from pilgrims, and the tension continued in the twentieth century as cathedrals reviewed their role. This tension became apparent in the 1980s when several cathedrals began charging for admission to their buildings. While there was sympathy for the financial problems experienced by cathedrals, many voices were raised in opposition:

> I recognize the enormous problems of financing cathedrals and that is why giving a donation when you leave is more appropriate. Grace is free, but it asks from us a response (perhaps costly). If our mission is about grace, I believe that our cathedrals must echo that, and entrance charges and grace seem to me to be saying opposite things.[7]

Theology and cathedrals

During the 1990s, theologians began to explore seriously the role of cathedrals in contemporary life. The dean of Durham, John Arnold, summarized this:

> Cathedrals witness, in an age of fragmentation and specialization, of analysis rather that synthesis, of division rather than cohesion, to a unity of purpose and a harmony of many different voices which can convey wholeness and healing to a generation which needs these things above all else.[8]

Similarly in *Flagships of the Spirit*, published in 1998, a series of essays focused on the expanding role of cathedrals, 'with the conviction that cathedrals have an essential part to play in the mission of the Church and in the life of contemporary society'.[9] Other theologians opened eyes to the importance of sacred space. John Inge, writing in 2003, speaks of 'sacramental encounters' in particular places like cathedrals:

> In such places the encounter is built into the story of the place for the Christian community as well as the individual, and this is how places become designated as holy. Holy places are thus associated with holy people to whom and in whom something of the glory of God has been revealed. The existence of such holy places should facilitate a sacramental perception and serve as a reminder that all time and place

belong to God in Christ – the part is set aside on behalf of, rather than instead of, the whole.[10]

The sociologist Grace Davie expanded horizons with her work. Writing in 2006 about the place of cathedrals in the religious life of Europe, she saw two things happening:

> the historic churches ... are losing their capacity to discipline the religious thinking of large sections of the population (especially the young). At the same time, the range of choice widens all the time as new forms of religion come into Europe from outside.[11]

Davie saw cathedrals as an ideal focus for those who 'believe but do not belong' – who have a spiritual awareness but do not feel the need to become full members of church structures.[12]

At the same time psychologists began to write about the importance of religious experience in the human psyche. Alister Hardy's Experience Research Unit at Oxford spent years analysing responses from a wide cross-section of society, not least those who visit cathedrals. His conclusion was that:

> It is surely this transcendental element that is fundamental: the feeling that there is a spiritual reality that appears to be beyond the conscious self with which the individual can have communion in one way or another – and whether spoken of as God or not – is indeed the most characteristic feature of the vast number of responses we have received.[13]

The church rediscovers healing

During the second half of the twentieth century the Church's role in healing was revived. Priests of broadly Anglo-Catholic outlook came to believe that the Church of England should be encouraged to restore the practices clearly used in the New Testament and during the patristic centuries. In *Anointing of the Sick in Scripture and Tradition*,[14] F. W. Puller argued for the restoration of anointing as a sacramental means by which God's healing grace is received, while Percy Dearmer provided in *The Parson's Handbook*[15] a liturgical form of a healing service with anointing. Similarly, the influential *Liturgy and Worship*, used by generations of ordinands, became a standard guide on the subject, through the essay of Charles Harris.[16] The formation of organizations like the Guild of St Raphael, the Guild of Health and the Divine Healing Mission encouraged anointing and a new awareness of the Church in the ministry of healing. The Churches' Council for Health and Healing (CCHH) was founded in 1944 with William Temple's support. Temple was very interested in the healing ministry. Addressing his diocesan conference in 1924, he said:

> You cannot read the Gospels and cut out the ministry of healing without tearing them to ribbons ... Nor can you draw a sharp line between what is physical and what is mental. The two merge in most baffling ways.

All this led to the setting up of the Archbishops' Commission in 1953. Since that official report, the ministry of healing has become a familiar and much used ministry in many parishes. It was given further official support through the influential report *A Time to Heal*.[17]

Arguably, this new emphasis on healing provided a further impetus for cathedrals to recognize afresh the place of shrines in their midst. Just as pilgrims had approached shrines of the saints during medieval times to seek health and wholeness, so now there seemed a natural revival of this ministry. Even if a shrine did not exist, cathedrals discovered the importance of a 'focus of prayer' – perhaps an icon – with opportunities to light candles and leave intercessions. This ministry reaches its most developed form at Walsingham, where the holy well within the shrine church is used daily by pilgrims and as the focus for healing, but cathedrals that have discovered new uses for their medieval shrine all speak of a real need for healing among the many thousands who come through their doors, and are responding in creative and effective ways.

The Church rediscovers the saints

We have seen how dioceses began to rediscover their indigenous saints and how these saints became increasingly celebrated in the liturgical life of dioceses. The 1976 report by the Liturgical Commission of the General Synod led to the greatly expanded number of commemorations associated with the Alternative Service Book (1980),[18] while other publications made provision for much wider celebration.[19] Although the Church of England had no official process of canonization, it was clear that a multitude of men and women were worthy of celebration and so now the calendar observed such diverse characters as Julian of Norwich, Junani Luwum, Oscar Romero, Thomas Traherne and Florence Nightingale. Led by the diocese of Truro in its calendars of local saints, other dioceses began to discover men and women who were special to their own area.

With the decline of daily worship in parish churches, it was the cathedrals that had the resources and schedules to put into practice these new liturgical possibilities.

Cathedrals rediscover ceremonial

In his work *Barchester*, Philip Barrett charts the development of cathedral worship during the nineteenth century. As the influence of the Oxford Movement developed, an increasing emphasis was placed on Holy Communion, with cathedrals instituting a weekly service at 8 a.m. as well as monthly choral celebrations.[20] However, cathedrals steered clear of anything that singled them out as beacons of catholic ceremonial.

Perhaps the most high-profile churchmanship issue in a cathedral came during the period 1931–35, when the reservation of the Sacrament caused huge upset in the diocese of Winchester. The 1928 Prayer Book had given limited possibilities for reservation, but its provisions pleased neither the Evangelicals nor the Anglo-Catholics. Cathedrals, on the whole, were of 'middling' churchmanship and ceremonial excesses were rare. In Winchester, however, there was something approaching uproar. Gordon Selwyn became dean in 1931 and petitioned the bishop, Theodore Wood, to allow reservation in a side chapel. This seems to have been accepted, but, on Wood's unexpected death and the appointment of his successor, Cyril Garbutt, the atmosphere changed. The new bishop was petitioned by representatives of the Church Association in the diocese, who objected to this 'grave irregularity'.[21] With other churches threatening to discontinue paying their quota over the issue, Bishop Garbutt became alarmed, writing to the dean:

> Unless there is an unanswerable case for perpetual reservation, you and the Chapter may find yourselves in the midst of a controversy which might sharply divide the diocese and gravely injure the cathedral.[22]

After four years' disagreement, the Chapter voted to discontinue the practice of reservation, the bishop stating that he had 'more anxiety over reservation at the cathedral than over any other problem since coming to the diocese'.[23]

The Winchester affair highlighted the concern felt in cathedrals over ceremonial matters. With high-profile disagreements between Anglo-Catholics and Evangelicals, cathedrals were seen as places strictly avoiding such controversy. New devotion to the saints seemed as distant as ever.

However, as the twentieth century progressed, there was a gradual increase in ceremonial used in cathedral worship. Reservation of the Blessed Sacrament was introduced in other cathedrals with much less controversy than at Winchester – at Lichfield, Ripon, St Albans and York during the 1950s. In Hereford, reservation was permitted in 1951 'but with the advice from the bishop that it was to be for the sick and aged only'.[24] Other cathedrals followed suit, including Gloucester and Westminster, both of which introduced reservation in a hanging pyx – a revival of a medieval practice. St Albans appears to have been one of the first cathedrals regularly to use eucharistic vestments, but the number increased with York (1940s), Ripon (1950s) and Oxford (1970s), so that by the time Westminster Abbey introduced vestments (1992) their use was almost universal. While the Sung Eucharist as a main act of worship on a Sunday found a place in a minority of cathedrals, by the 1990s this again was almost universal.

Incense was used in cathedrals very rarely at the beginning of the twentieth century but is now found in the majority although with a varied frequency, from Oxford using it only a handful of times to Lincoln using it over half the year and St Albans 60–70 times a year. When introduced in Hereford, a Chapter Act of 1981 noted: 'It will have been noticed that, on great occasions incense is now used and it is hoped that no one will find this ancient custom at all questionable.'[25]

Other devotional practices can now be found in many cathedrals – Blessing of the Oils on Maundy Thursday, the full observance of Holy Week ceremonies, the Sacrament of Reconciliation, the daily Eucharist, six candlesticks on the high altar (York, Wakefield, Hereford), the use of holy water, the celebration of Requiems on All Souls' Day, statues and icons, the ringing of the Angelus, and even Eucharistic Adoration and Benediction at several (St Albans, Guildford and Hereford) may be found.

In short, during the twentieth century, cathedrals began to embrace the full panoply of all that the catholic tradition could offer by way of ceremonial practices and thus made the renaissance of shrines and their use much easier and more natural.[26]

Cathedrals and ecumenism

As the twentieth century progressed, cathedrals became more and more aware of the importance of links with other churches, and this in turn led to their willingness to embrace ceremonial practices previously held to be unacceptable in the Church of England.

Cathedrals opened their doors to local Roman Catholic communities. We have seen how the Catholic community at Canterbury is regularly welcomed into Canterbury Cathedral and vice versa, and there are frequent celebrations of mass at the shrine of St Alban. Many cathedrals now have Ecumenical Canons or Ecumenical Companions – a tangible way of showing how cathedral ministry and worship can transcend denominational boundaries.

Notes

1 See H. C. N. Williams, 1964, *20th Century Cathedral: An examination of the role of cathedrals in the strategy of the Church in a changing pattern of a twentieth century community*, London: Hodder and Stoughton, pp. 78–9.

2 *English Cathedrals and Tourism: Problems and Opportunities*, a report by the English Tourist Board, 1979.

3 M. Shackley, 2001, *Managing Sacred Sites: Service Provision and Visitor Experience*, London: Thomson Learning.

4 Shackley, *Managing Sacred Sites*, p. 192.

5 *Heritage and Renewal: The Report of the Archbishops' Commission on Cathedrals*, 1994, Church House Publishing.

6 *Heritage and Renewal*, 1.

7 S. Bessant, diocesan missioner of Blackburn. See Minutes of the meeting of the General Synod of the Church of England held on 25 February 2004, in *General Synod – Report of Proceedings*, vol. 34, no. 1, pp. 111–18, 116–17.

8 J. Arnold, 'Cathedrals and God's Word and Life', in I. M. MacKenzie (ed.), 1996, *Cathedrals Now: Their Use and Place in Society*, Norwich: Canterbury Press, pp. 81–94.

9 S. Platten and C. Lewis (eds), 1998, *Flagships of the Spirit: Cathedrals in Society*, London: Darton, Longman & Todd, p. xv.

10 J. Inge, 2003, *A Christian Theology of Place*, Aldershot and Burlington VT: Ashgate Publishing, p. 90.

11 G. Davie, 2006, 'A post-script: The place of cathedrals in the religious life of Europe', in S. Platten and C. Lewis (eds), *Dreaming Spires? Cathedrals in a New Age*, London: SPCK, pp. 145–56.

12 See G. Davie, 1994, *Religion in Modern Britain since 1945: Believing without Belonging*, Malden, MA, Oxford and Carlton, Victoria: Blackwell Publishing.

13 A. Hardy, 1979, *The Spiritual Nature of Man: A Study of Contemporary Religious Experience*, 1997, Oxford: The Religious Experience Research Centre, Westminster College, p. 132.

14 F. W. Puller, 1904, *Anointing of the Sick in Scripture and Tradition*, London: SPCK.

15 P. Dearmer, 1907, *The Parson's Handbook*, London: Oxford University Press.

16 C. Harris, 'Visitation of the Sick', in W. K. Lowther Clarke (ed.), 1932, *Liturgy and Worship*, London: SPCK, pp. 472–540.

17 Archbishops' Council, 2000, *A Time to Heal*, London: Church House Publishing.

18 *The Calendar, Lectionary and Rules to Order the Service 1976*, A Report by the Liturgical Commission of the General Synod of the Church of England, GS 292.

19 See M. Draper (ed.), 1982, *The Cloud of Witnesses: A Companion to the Lesser Festivals and Holydays of the Alternative Service Book 1980*, London: Collins. Br Tristram (ed.), 1997, *Exciting Holiness: Collects and Readings for the Festivals and Lesser Festivals of the Calendar of the Church of England*, Norwich: Canterbury Press.

20 See P. Barrett, 1993, *Barchester: English Cathedral Life of the 19th Century*, London: SPCK, pp. 138–9.

21 See T. E. Daykin, 'Reservation of the Sacrament at Winchester Cathedral, 1931–1935', in R. N. Swanson (ed.), 1990, *Continuity and Change in Christian Worship: Studies in Church History* (35), Woodbridge: Boydell Press, pp. 464–77.

22 Daykin, 'Reservation', pp. 464–77.

23 Daykin 'Reservation', pp. 464–77.

24 Hereford Cathedral Chapter Acts, 6 February, 1951.

25 Hereford Cathedral Chapter Acts, 6 March, 1981.

26 I am very grateful to the deans and precentors of the following cathedrals and churches who kindly assisted me in providing information leading to this conclusion – Gloucester, Lichfield, Lincoln, Oxford, Peterborough, Ripon, St Albans, Wakefield, York, Westminster Abbey.

7

Restored shrines

St Albans – a major development of pilgrimage in an English cathedral

Shrine of St Alban, restored 1993

The shrine pedestal of St Alban remained untouched until 1991, when it was taken down for conservation and restoration. The site was excavated in 1991 and the pedestal reconstructed in 1992–93 using additional fragments, discovered since the shrine had been reassembled in 1872. Missing pieces, such as the surrounding shafts, flying buttresses and pinnacles, were supplied in cast resin. A canopy designed and embroidered by Suellen Pedley and the sisters of All Saints convent in Oxford was placed on the restored pedestal in the position it occupied from about 1308 until 1539 by the twelfth-century chests containing the relics of St Alban. The restored shrine was dedicated on 6 May 1993 by the bishop of St Albans and the then dean, the Very Revd

Peter Moore, in the presence of Queen Elizabeth the Queen Mother. Thus, with the aid of modern scholarship and technology the shrine was reconstructed to celebrate the twelve-hundredth anniversary of the Saxon foundation of the abbey. The order of service at the dedication emphasized the beauty of the restoration and yet the 'emptiness' of the shrine:

> The very absence of the saint's body, the empty tomb which the shrine now represents, a wound healed but still present from the strife of the Reformation, all speak of the power of the risen Christ; for it is from his wounds that healing flows. The paradox remains – nothing limits God, we have no abiding city; and yet there is nothing for which we long more eagerly, for it is our hope of heaven.[1]

Several years later, in 2002, the cathedral received a gift from the church of St Pantaleon in Cologne – a priceless relic from their own ancient reliquary. The relic, a shoulder-bone, was installed in the shrine at St Albans by the auxiliary bishop of Cologne in a special service, As one bystander on the occasion remarked, 'Ah, so St Alban has come home, then.'

A great deal is made of the feast of St Alban in June each year, with a weekend festival and a great procession from the town to the shrine, featuring giant 'puppets' which re-enact the story of Alban. There is a daily Eucharist at the shrine and the shrine is used for mass by the local Roman Catholic congregation as well as by Eastern Orthodox, Free Church and German Lutheran communities.

St David

The shrine of St David was magnificently restored in the period from 2010 and now stands as a major example of how a shrine can find new use and spirituality.

We have seen how the remains of the shrine were to be found on the north side of the presbytery of St Davids Cathedral – a two-sided shrine protruding into the north choir aisle.

Both sides of the shrine have been enriched with the placing of icons – on the presbytery side, icons of St David, St Andrew and St Patrick, and on the aisle side, icons of St Justinian and St Non. The icons, by Sarah Crisp, replicate those known to have been on the shrine in the Middle Ages.

Shrine of St David, St Davids Cathedral

Above the shrine is a richly decorated canopy, while below it are found three niches, formerly for kneeling. These now contain two reliquaries, reputed to contain the remains of St David and St Justinian, together with a replica of a Celtic 'Bangau' bell.

The restored shrine was dedicated on 1 March 2012 by the bishop of St Davids; later in the year, on 24 March, the shrine was visited by Dr Rowan Williams, archbishop of Canterbury.

The shrine is now a focus for prayer, healing and pilgrimage. Prayers are held at the site every Friday at 12 noon and the whole cathedral feels transformed by the honour now done to the patron saint in such a colourful, imaginative and authentic way.[2]

Lichfield – St Chad

By 1931 it had become customary to put the St Chad's Gospels on display behind the reredos of the high altar on 2 March each year. The physical site of the medieval shrine east of the high altar was marked, modestly, with a stone slab, commemorating the nineteen-hundredth anniversary of the death of Chad and was unveiled by the duchess of Gloucester and dedicated by the archbishops of Canterbury and York.[3]

Shrine of St Chad, Lichfield Cathedral

Further embellishment of the shrine was added through the commissioning of an icon of St Chad in 1998, with provision for the lighting of candles nearby. A final part of the renaissance of St Chad's shrine has been spoken about for some years. In the late 1990s plans were discussed for the commissioning of a shrine-like structure:

> The shrine is the natural focus of personal prayer here in the cathedral and we want to enhance that, possibly by commissioning a new shrine

that could be suspended from the ceiling, able to be raised when we hold concerts in the Lady chapel and visible in its regular place, from the west end of the cathedral, seen above and complementing the present reredos.[4]

On the departure of Dean Wright in 1999, he noted that 'plans for the shrine need firming up and implementing',[5] and at the time of writing discussions continue between the present dean, Adrian Dorber, and the administrator of St Chad's Roman Catholic Cathedral as to possible future co-operation whereby, when the shrine is restored, part of the collection of relics now at St Chad's cathedral might find a new home in a restored shrine at Lichfield Cathedral.[6]

Thus, in this last aspiration, we see in a comparison of devotions at Lichfield Cathedral and St Chad's Roman Catholic Cathedral an interesting reversal of roles. St Chad's started out as an entirely relic-focused devotion, the shrine containing relics of Chad, important for the authentication of local Catholic credentials in the Midlands; other 'remembrance' elements such as processions and pilgrimages came later. The Anglican devotion, at Lichfield Cathedral, by comparison, began with 'remembrance' elements (lectures, annual services, images in the cathedral fabric) and only later focused attention on physical interpretations of the cult (site of shrine and the possibility of a relic).

Ely – St Etheldreda

Rekindled devotion to Etheldreda was slower to re-establish itself at Ely than had been the case with Chad at Lichfield, but by 1914 Etheldreda was celebrated in cathedral services on 17 October (the feast of Etheldreda's translation), and later in the century observances were held on 23 June, the date of her death. From 1928, honorary canons were invited to join the October celebrations, and in 1954 the County War Memorial Chapel, east of the high altar, was dedicated to her and a life-sized statue installed there.

After James Bentham's less than flattering description of the medieval shrine, there appears to have been no further description until that of Dean Stubbs in his twentieth edition of the *Cathedral Handbook*,[7] which includes a description from Bentham of the medieval shrine and shows on a plan the site of the former shrine.

The site of the shrine was marked during the 1950s by four gilded candlesticks,[8] but by 1968 the cleaning of them had proved too

Site of the shrine of St Etheldreda, Ely Cathedral

expensive and the cathedral architects, Purcell Miller Tritton, were commissioned to design new candlesticks for the site. In 1969, the site of the shrine was marked by an incised slab carved by David Kinnersley and the stone surrounded by the four new candlesticks.

Durham – St Cuthbert

In 1542, Cuthbert's body was reburied after its exhumation at the Dissolution – possibly the only pre-Reformation saint (apart from Edward the Confessor) whose body remained intact after the destruction of shrines. Legends abound – was Cuthbert's body spirited away to a secret location, while his grave in Durham Cathedral was filled with the body of a Durham monk?

In 1827, under the auspices of James Raine, a fiercely Protestant clergyman, the grave was opened, possibly, it is thought, to allay speculations of an alternative burial on the site. Inside the stone grave, onlookers found the remains of three wooden coffins, one of which proved to be pieces of the original chest made for the body when it was disinterred in 698. A complete skeleton, swathed in the remains of fine shrouds of either silk or linen, was found in the tomb along with many bones heaped together. The skeleton was carefully removed and it appeared to have undergone no decomposition in the coffin. A few treasures that had escaped in 1539 were found – a portable altar, an ivory comb and a magnificent gold pectoral cross encrusted with precious stones, a wonderful example of delicate sixth-century crafts-manship. These artefacts are all now on display in the cathedral.[9] In 1899 further excavation uncarthed fragments of masonry which had been reutilized in 1542. These were placed as a ledge around the tomb slab in the feretory. The feretory space itself, used for many years for the storage of discarded statuary, was gradually brought back into use. During the 1930s, the Friends of the cathedral restored seventeenth-century woodwork around the area, and by 1947 Comper's design for a canopy had been realized. This shows Christ in Glory with the four evangelists and, together with four huge Comper candlesticks, provides a great dignity to the shrine today.

Shrine of St Cuthbert, Durham Cathedral

Further embellishments were made – a fourteenth-century statue of Cuthbert, holding the head of Oswald, was introduced, and in 2001 two banners by Thetis Blacker were added; one is of an eagle feeding the hungry Cuthbert with a salmon. Made by the batik method, these contemporary banners used wax previously burned in public worship at various candle stands in the cathedral.

The feasts of Cuthbert, on 20 March and 4 September, are kept with great solemnity in the cathedral; there are regular prayers at the shrine and the Eucharist is celebrated regularly at a modern altar installed during the 1980s.[10]

Durham – the Venerable Bede

Shrine of the Venerable Bede, Durham Cathedral

In 1542, Bede's body was reinterred in the cathedral, with the present raised tomb chest constructed during the early nineteenth century. The shrine area in the Galilee Chapel was further enriched with a panel depicting words by Bede, and installed in memory of Dean Allington and his wife Hester. The work by Frank Roper is of metal, designed by George Pace (1970). The Bede window is by Alan Younger, installed in

1973 to mark the thirteen-hundredth anniversary of the birth of Bede.[11]

Chester – St Werburgh

The shrine of St Werburgh served as a base for the bishop's throne until the Victorian restoration of the cathedral. In 1888, under the direction of the architect Arthur Blomfield, the pieces of the shrine were reassembled and placed in the retro-choir. The shrine now stands in the entrance to the Lady Chapel – one of the largest shrine structures remaining in England. A delicate statue of St Werbergh was placed in the middle of the shrine in 1993.

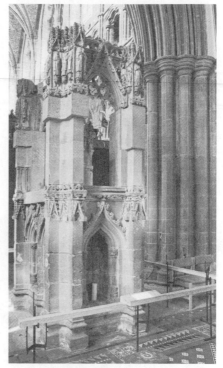

Shrine of St Werburgh, Chester Cathedral

Winchester – St Swithun

After its destruction, the shrine of St Swithun was never forgotten in the cathedral but it was only in 1936 that the site of the final shrine at the east end of the cathedral was marked out by a strip of wood bearing the following inscription (in Latin):

All of Swithun that could die lay here enshrined. Hither came the faithful, not of one age or clime, to honour him with prayers and gifts. A later age laid rude hands upon his relics, but could not touch his fame. All that is of God is safe in God.

In 1962 Dean Gibbs-Smith announced:

The Friends have also undertaken to erect a beautiful tomb-grille in wrought iron, with a rich canopy over the site of the shrine of St. Swithun; this is now being made to the designs of Mr. Brian Thomas in consultation with our architect, Mr. Carpenter Turner. This embellishment of the shrine will provide the Cathedral with a new work of art in deliberate contrast with the two beautiful chantries on either side of it, and it will be ready for the celebrations on St. Swithun's Day, 15th July.[12]

Shrine of St Swithun, Winchester Cathedral

This structure was very forward-looking at the time and placed Winchester at the forefront of cathedrals who were taking their saints' shrines seriously. The rich fabric canopy was particularly fine, although by the late twentieth century it had deteriorated and has now been removed, leaving the metal structure on its own.

During the twentieth century exciting discoveries were made and enough fragments of the shrine were found to have survived for a reconstruction to be made. They were discovered in a variety of locations. The first piece to be found was removed by Dean Kitchin in 1885 from the infill of the 'Pilgrim's Door'. Then in 1907, three fragments of what may have been a cornice were discovered; finally, during the 1990s, fragments of worked Purbeck marble with delicate carving were discovered in the footings of a collapsed wall on the site of the monastic dormitory, together with elements of what was clearly a niche in the structure. All this enabled a three-dimensional computer model of the shrine to be created, showing the prayer niches, with detailing similar to that in the nearby chantry of Cardinal Beaufort.

Shrine of St Swithun – computer reconstruction

In the long term, it is hoped that the shrine may be reassembled in its original position in the retro-choir, thus bringing to eight the number of saints' shrines that have been put together again in modern times.

Westminster Abbey – St Edward the Confessor

After the Reformation, the space around St Edward's shrine was still used, not least for coronations, when a table was set up, designated in the rubrics as 'St Edward's altar', on which certain pieces of regalia were placed during the ceremony. A more substantial altar was placed in the chapel in 1902, in time for the coronation of Edward VII. On this the coronation oil was hallowed on 9 August and the following day the Eucharist was celebrated there, probably for the first time in 340 years. After this, the Eucharist was always celebrated on the shrine altar on St Edward's day, 13 October, and a tradition developed of a Roman Catholic celebration of mass at the same festival.

From 2005, the year of the millennium of the Confessor's birth, the use of the shrine developed under the leadership of Dean John Hall, and 13 October became the main Feast of Dedication (traditionally, this had been kept on 28 December). The festival was observed with a series of lectures, concerts and other events that helped to focus attention on the Confessor's significance.

At the shrine now, the Eucharist is celebrated every Tuesday and each day during the 'octave' of the feast of St Edward on 13 October. The feast itself is observed with great solemnity, including a Solemn Eucharist and Evensong and a major gathering of pilgrims. There are regular pilgrim prayers at the shrine and a tradition is developing of churches in and beyond the diocese coming from their own churches on pilgrimage to the shrine.

Shrine of St Edward the Confessor, Westminster Abbey.

Significant visits to the shrine in recent years have included that in 2007 of the Ecumenical Patriarch and the archbishop of Canterbury, who prayed at the shrine and censed it during Evensong. In 2010, Pope Benedict and the archbishop prayed together at the shrine during the pope's visit to England.

Salisbury – St Osmund

Devotion to St Osmund is focused on the Trinity Chapel at the east end of the cathedral. There are two sites – the saint's actual grave, under a black slab in the middle of the chapel, and the stone shrine, with apertures for pilgrims to gain access to the relics (this structure is now on the south side of the Trinity Chapel). The grave slab dates from St Osmund's canonization in 1457 and has constantly burning candles at each end.

Tomb/shrine of St Osmund, Salisbury Cathedral

York – St William

By 1541 both shrines had been destroyed and the stonework buried in various locations around the Minster. Over the years, a large number of these have come to light, both during the eighteenth and nineteenth centuries and more recently in 1927–28. Some fragments strayed as far as the gardens adjoining Clifford's Tower in the castle. These fragments have been reassembled and are on public display at the Yorkshire Museum – they show a remarkable range of intricate carving, including a full statue of St Margaret, secular figures such as a crossbowman and evidence of the prayer niches with which both shrines appear to have been surrounded. The original coffin – probably a reused Roman sarcophagus – survives and has been replaced in the Minster crypt, where it serves as a focus for devotion to St William, along with a mosaic of the saint, opportunities for lighting candles and an altar. The shrine is regularly visited by pilgrims, especially the Carmelite community, which gathers for an annual mass and pilgrimage day at about the time of the feast of St William, 8 June.[13]

Tomb/shrine of St William, York Minster

Lincoln – St Hugh

It appears that, although the principal shrine was destroyed without trace, the fabric of the head shrine survived into the mid-seventeenth century; Bishop Sanderson recorded that there was, in 1640, 'a beautiful shrine of St Hugh of great height in pyramidal fashion'.[14] Certainly the head shrine was drawn by William Dugdale in the seventeenth century, at which time the reliquary appears to be have been intact.[15]

The cult of St Hugh lapsed, but in the nineteenth century there was a revival of interest. In 1883 the Carthusian monastery of Parkminster, Sussex, was completed and dedicated to St Hugh, the only Catholic Charterhouse to be founded in England since the Reformation and still one of the largest religious houses in the world. In Lincoln itself, there was renewed interest. Edmund Venables, precentor of the cathedral and a noted medievalist, wrote extensively on the subject and threw light on the original position of the shrine:

> The supposed site of the shrine (destroyed at the Reformation) is indicated by the black marble table bearing an inscription, erected by Bishop Fuller on the north side of the Presbytery during the general restoration of the cathedral after the Restoration (1667–1673). It is impossible to believe that the place is correctly assigned. The almost universal rule was that the shrine of the chief saint of any great church should be in the centre of the space behind the high altar and elevated so as to be visible above the reredos, that by gazing upon it the hearts of the priests celebrating at the altar might be raised to emulate the holy man's virtues. Of this arrangement we have existing examples in the shrine of St Edward the Confessor at Westminster Abbey and St Alban at St Albans; and we know that the shrines of St William at York, St Thomas at Canterbury and St Etheldreda at Ely occupied the same position.[16]

Further scholarly work was undertaken by Venables on the architectural history of the shrine and the profile of St Hugh was raised through the decision in 1902 to install a stained-glass window of the life of St Hugh above the Fleming Chantry.[17] The appeal described 'a project which the Dean and Chapter have in view for preserving in the cathedral the memory of St Hugh's Day, 1900, and at the same time adding (they hope) to the beauty of the Angel Choir, which was built as his shrine'.[18] The window, executed by the craftsman Henry Holiday, was dedicated by the bishop of Lincoln on St Hugh's day, 1902, and depicts eight scenes from St Hugh's life. In his address the bishop, starting from a sentence of Sir James Paget, 'spoke of the foundation of the saintly character as being laid in the common virtues, negative and positive, of daily life'.[19]

The question of St Hugh's body was confronted in 1921. It was alleged that St Hugh's first burial place had been discovered empty in 1886 and that at the Reformation his body may have been reinterred in the cathedral Chapter House, although this theory has never been proven.[20] Devotion to St Hugh continued throughout the twentieth century, one writer extolling the influence such devotion had on the life of the cathedral:

> Thus, though the old order has changed, there rises again today from these chapels the voice of praise and prayer and intercession for the temporal and spiritual needs of the world, in the daily offering of the church's worship, linking the living and the dead in one fellowship through the ages.[21]

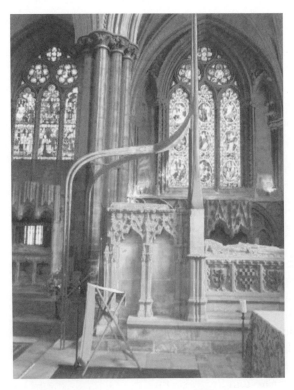

Shrine of St Hugh, Lincoln Cathedral

A focus for the most recent revival of interest in St Hugh was provided in 1986, the eight-hundredth anniversary of Hugh's enthronement as bishop of Lincoln, when a series of events was organized to mark the occasion. As a lasting memorial of the anniversary year, the Dean and Chapter commissioned the sculptor David Poston to create a modern-istic canopy of bronze-coated stainless steel to surround the battered remnants of the head shrine. The design recalls the swan with which Hugh established a relationship at Stow.[22] It is a twentieth-century interpretation of the cult, focusing minds on the gentle piety of the saint and the natural world, where he found spiritual peace.[23]

Chichester – St Richard

Shrine of St Richard, Chichester Cathedral

During the nineteenth century there was increased interest in St Richard. Antiquarian guides make mention of the shrine,[24] stained-glass windows commemorating the saint were introduced and in 1894 a statue of St Richard was placed in St Richard's porch. In 1905 the shrine platform itself was reinstated.[25] During the 1930s, an altar was placed on the raised platform behind the high altar – the site of the shrine. *The Chichester Customary* of Dean Duncan Jones[26] describes ceremonial taking place on the feast of the Translation of St Richard on 16 July, together with illustrations showing choreography.

In 1953 there was a pageant of the seven-hundredth anniversary of St Richard's death and at this time two hymns were written in honour of St Richard. Several of these were based on St Richard's Prayer:

Day by day,
Dear Lord, of thee three things I pray:
To see thee more clearly,
Love thee more dearly,
Follow thee more nearly,
Day by day.

One found its way into *Songs of Praise*, with a tune by Somervell.[27]

A Guild of St Richard was founded in 1944 – a young communicants group, with an emphasis on spiritual and social life.

During the 1970s, a large tapestry was placed behind St Richard's altar. It is by German artist Ursula Benker-Schirmer, and is woven with biblical symbols linked to St Richard's life. Nearby is an icon of St Richard with votive candle stand. This was given in 2003, the seven-hundred-and-fiftieth anniversary of the saint's death. It is by Sergei Fyodorov, and shows St Richard in his episcopal vestments, his hand raised in blessing towards the viewer, and with Christ offering prayer in heaven. When the icon was dedicated it 'went on pilgrimage', resting at Dover where Richard died, and arriving at the cathedral via visits to churches, hospitals and schools *en route*.

There has been a growing interest in the use of relics associated with shrines, and in 1990 a relic of St Richard was presented to the cathedral. It has a fascinating history. There had been a long-standing link between Chichester and La Lucerne in south-west Normandy, where an arm of St Richard appears to have been lodged from about 1276. In 1594, La Lucerne was pillaged and the St Richard relic was rescued. By 1634 there was evidence of a new reliquary, but at the French Revolution it was kept in secret by the local priest. The relic was discovered during a restoration of La Lucerne in 1987. After being presented to Chichester, it was received by the cathedral, placed in a casket and interred in the floor of the retro-choir, on St Richard's day 1991. The marble plaque has the following inscription:

In hoc olim stabat
Feretrum Sancti Ricardi Cicestrensis
AD MCCLCCVI EXSTRUCTUM
IUSSU AUTEM REGIS HENRICI VIII AD MDXXXVIII
DURUTUM ET SUBLATUM
BEATI MITES BEATI MUNDO CORDI

In this place once stood the shrine of Saint Richard of Chichester
Constructed in 1276 but on the order of King Henry VIII
in 1538 demolished and taken away.
Blessed are the Meek. Blessed are the pure in heart.

A further restoration of the shrine took place in 2012, with new candle stands and furniture, given in memory of Bishop Eric Kempe.

Oxford – St Frideswide

Shrine of St Frideswide, Christ Church, Oxford

Pieces of the medieval shrine were discovered in the 1870s and, together with further pieces discovered during a restoration of the cloister in 1985, were reassembled in the Latin Chapel on the north side of the cathedral and dedicated in 2002. In a sermon preached during that year, Canon Henry Mayr-Harting took the opportunity to interpret the use of the shrine in the church of the Middle Ages and today.

So why were people drawn to the shrine? Partly, I suppose, because they knew that, if they were not going to encounter a conjurer in St Frideswide, they would at least be received with sympathy and understanding by the clergy and the congregation ... To my mind it does not matter much whether anything about Frideswide, beyond the undoubted fact of her existence, is reliably known or not. And the reason why it does not matter is because of the communion of saints.

A sixth-century Gallic writer, Gregory of Tours, maintained that whatever was said of one of the saints in their glory, could equally be said of all the others ... what mattered was our closeness to the communion of saints rather than to individual celebrities, our closeness to the City of God as a city, as a whole society.[28]

Near to the shrine is the medieval watching chamber and behind is the Victorian St Frideswide Window, created by Edward Burne-Jones in 1858. The top panel shows a ship of souls carrying Frideswide to heaven, and the flower-shaped windows below that show the Tree of Knowledge and the Tree of Life. The remaining 16 panels depict scenes from the saint's life.

Dorchester – St Birinus

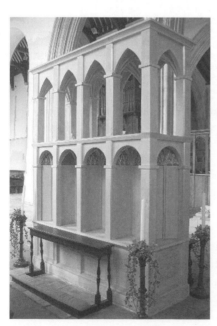

A fourteenth-century chronicler, Higden, records that a new and magnificently carved marble shrine was made in 1320. It was destroyed at the Reformation, and in the nineteenth century fragments of a fourteenth-century canopied shrine were found built into the blocking of a doorway in the north transept. They consisted of elaborate rib-vaulting of freestone and were reused in the present shrine reconstruction, designed in 1964 by F. Russell Cox. The reconstruction gives an excellent glimpse of the size and scale of such shrines and has become the focus of renewed devotion to St Birinus in Dorchester Abbey.

Shrine of St Birinus, Dorchester.

Our Lady of Walsingham

Shrine of Our Lady of Walsingham, Holy House

Walsingham is now a place of pilgrimage unparalleled in Britain. About 350,000 visitors and pilgrims come to this sacred place each year, shared between Anglican, Catholic and Orthodox believers.

Roman Catholics continued their devotions at the Slipper Chapel. In 1934 the shrine was elevated to the status of the Roman Catholic National Shrine of Our Lady, and is the centre of a new festival in the Catholic calendar, the Feast of Our Lady of Walsingham. The shrine complex now includes a large, modern Chapel of Reconciliation, which can seat up to 350.

The Anglican shrine, having been re-established in the 1930s, has grown in influence and stability over the years. The brick shrine church provides a complex covering for the Holy House – effectively a shrine chapel in the middle of a much larger church. The Holy House contains the statue of Our Lady of Walsingham, a replica of the medieval carving burned by Henry VIII. The shrine church, with its 15 side chapels representing the Mysteries of the Rosary, also contains a Russian Orthodox chapel, with iconostasis, and incorporates in its south-west corner a holy well, frequently used by pilgrims. Next to the shrine church is a large visitor centre, capable of accommodating 200 pilgrims, together with refectory and cafe. The gardens have been developed into a devotional area, with Stations of the Cross.

Many pilgrimages take place during the year – individual, parish, youth, diocesan – but the largest of all, the National Pilgrimage, takes place on the Bank Holiday at the end of May.[29]

St Melangell at Pennant Melangell

One of the most interesting and engaging restorations of a shrine and its cult can be seen at Pennant Melangell – a tiny Norman church deep in the hills of Montgomeryshire.

The shrine was probably demolished during the period 1538–53, although the remoteness of the site, as well as evidence that the diocese of St Asaph was issuing proclamations relating to the removal of relics as late as 1561, suggests that the shrine may have survived into the second half of the sixteenth century.

The legendary site of Melangell's grave was within a small annexe to the main body of the church known as the Cell-y-Bedd, or 'cell of the grave'. This was covered in the post-Reformation period with a structure that became a schoolroom or vestry.

Little is recorded of Melangell's cult, but during conservation works in 1958 the floor was excavated and the footings of an earlier Cell-y-Bedd was discovered. By this date, various carved stones had been discovered – some in the walls of the church and the stone porch over the lychgate which were identified as parts of the twelfth-century shrine. Several of the pieces were removed from their locations and reassembled in the post-medieval Cell-y-Bedd to a design by Ralegh Radford.

The condition of the church itself deteriorated and there was a threat to remove the entire building to St Fagan's, the Museum of Welsh Culture at Cardiff. However, thanks to the enthusiasm of the then incumbent, the Revd Paul Davies, and his wife Evelyn, a campaign was launched to save the church. In the course of the restoration that followed the appeal, the Cell-y-Bedd was rebuilt on its medieval foundations and the original grave of the saint appropriately marked. Of even greater significance, the pieces of the Romanesque shrine were reassembled in the chancel of the church.[30] What we now have is a shrine surviving in a form that is unique in Britain and rare in Europe. Roughly half is renewed, with surfaces being left blank to distinguish them from the original stones, with their interlaced patterning. The chest supposedly containing the saint's relics is raised on round columns and arches, crowned with a steep gable and drooping crockets.

Shrine of St Melangell, Pennant Melangell

At the same time as the church and shrine were restored (1988–90), a nearby house was converted into a healing centre and the shrine became associated with a ministry of wholeness and healing. Today, the area below the shrine is frequently covered with prayer cards placed there by pilgrims and the Eucharist is celebrated at a stone altar attached to the west end of the shrine itself. The church retains a fifteenth-century screen, which has a carved frieze depicting St Melangell, the prince with his horn, and the hare.

Hereford – the changing fortunes of a saint's shrine, 1850–2008

During the early nineteenth century, the shrine of St Thomas continued as an antiquarian oddity, exciting interest as an example of medieval stonework. During the major restoration of the cathedral building (1857–63) it received attention, being taken apart and reconstructed with a brick interior. In a later restoration, a piece of slate was found, presumably left by one of the stonemasons, inside the stone base. It reads:

> Robt Berridge
> Castor
> Nr Peterborough
> Northamptonshire
> June 26 1861
> Gone to the dogs
> When this is found.

Interest was aroused during the 1930s, with various scholarly articles on the likely appearance of the medieval shrine,[31] and the transept was set out as a chapel during the 1950s with two altars relating to the shrine.

A key development occurred in the late 1970s, when there was a scheme to interpret the shrine in a contemporary manner. What emerged was the 'Nimbus', a metal creation by David Watkins, which was dedicated in 1981. David Watkins describes the Nimbus thus:

> The shape and position of the tomb suggested a horizontal, overhead object, which in turn suggested the symbolism of floating in space, and defying gravity. The object was visualized as a marker in space and position of the saint, to be seen from a distance, but understood only from close quarters ... In my mind, the overall form is a metaphor of a sound – a chord or mantra – suggesting calm and repose.[32]

The then dean of Hereford, Norman Rathbone, wrote enthusiastically about the concept and saw it in spiritual and mystical terms:

> Above the shrine of St Thomas of Hereford, in the north transept of this cathedral, now hangs an ornament fashioned in shining and coloured metals which the craftsman who devised and made it has called a nimbus. It is not itself a source of light illuminating the tomb

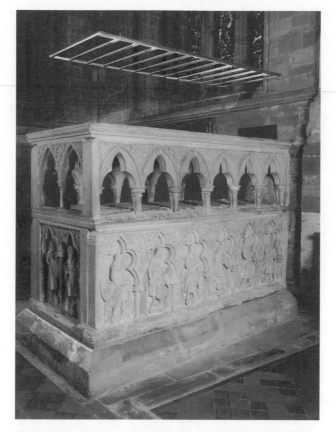

Shrine of St Thomas of Hereford with 'Nimbus' (1981)

of the Saint as a precious object to be admired by visiting eyes. It re-
flects a hidden light which issues from the tomb itself. In a remarkable
and imaginative way it suggests the radiance of sanctity, that spiritual
brightness and supernatural light which shines upon the world in the
lives of holy men and women. The radiance of holiness like the odour
of sanctity is the symbol of the divine presence, a grace and power
manifest in the saint. Moses, descending from Sinai, must veil his face
to conceal its mysterious and perilous brightness. Stephen's judges
saw his face shining as an angel's; and the corpse of Hereford's own
martyr and saint, Ethelbert, was accompanied by strange lights …[33]

By the 1990s, the shrine base itself was showing signs of deterioration
and a major archaeological survey and reconstruction were undertaken.
The shrine base was dismantled, studied and reassembled, with opportunities taken for scholarly reassessment of this extraordinary survival.[34]

Archaeological restoration of shrine (1997)

The refurbishment 2005–08

There the shrine base stood in the north transept of the cathedral – a beautiful example of medieval craftsmanship, but, with the growing development of pilgrimage in the cathedral, something more engaging and attractive was clearly needed.

The shrine refurbishment was carried out under the direction of cathedral architect Robert Kilgour, supported by craftsmen Stephen Florence, Peter Murphy and Neil Lossock. The newly refurbished shrine was brought into use on 8 November 2008 and dedicated by the bishop of Hereford, the Right Revd Anthony Priddis. A relic of St Thomas was handed over to the bishop by the Abbots of Downside and Belmont, symbolizing the new-found unity that the shrine expresses.

The following describes the various sections of the project and the rationale behind each.

Wall hangings

Around the walls of the north transept are mounted rich hangings depicting the life of Thomas Cantilupe in 12 scenes. The hangings are designed by the late Terry Hamaton and made by Brendon and Julie Quinn of Croft Design in Much Wenlock. The ironwork supports have wolf-headed finials (a nod towards the name of Cantilupe, which means 'the wolf').

Shrine of St Thomas of Hereford (2008)

Canopy

A new canopy, given by Sir Roy Strong, is placed on the medieval shrine base and gives an impression of the former appearance of the shrine, with all its vivid colour. The canopy has a panel at its east end depicting the saints associated with Hereford: in the centre is the Blessed Virgin Mary, the cathedral's principal patron, holding the Christ-child; on one side of Our Lady we see St Ethelbert the King, the cathedral's secondary patron, and on the other side St John the Baptist, the cathedral's parochial saint. In the corners we see depictions of St Thomas of Hereford on the left, kneeling with his wolf (or 'lupus') peeping from behind him; and on the right, St Thomas of Canterbury ('the other Thomas') with whom the Hereford Thomas is often linked in iconography. In front of the Blessed Virgin are two angels holding a depiction of the Mappa Mundi: there is a theory that the Mappa Mundi was originally associated with the Shrine of St Thomas – the map of wonders functioning, like the shrine itself, as a draw for pilgrims.

At the east end of the canopy is a further icon on the apex, this time depicting Christ in glory, surrounded by local characters, including the donors (Roy Strong and Julia Trevelyan Oman) and even the bishop and dean!

Reliquary

Beneath the canopy is a brass and glass reliquary, which contains a small relic of St Thomas of Hereford. At the destruction of the shrine, Cantilupe's relics found their way into the homes of devout Catholics. We hear of one relic being associated, from the 1670s, with the shrine at Holywell in North Wales, while the skull, which was rediscovered during the nineteenth century in the monastery of Lambspring in Germany, is now in a reliquary at Downside Abbey. The relic in the shrine today is associated with the Holywell relic and has been in the care of Stonyhurst College in Lancashire since the 1830s. The tiny relic is placed in a silver heart-shaped reliquary dating from the mid-seventeenth century and engraved with the sacred monogram.

A shrine reconstructed – St Ethelbert at Hereford

Hereford Cathedral's ancient dedication is to St Ethelbert the King – a saint not to be confused with Canterbury's Ethelbert of Kent, who was the first Christian Anglo-Saxon king. Hereford's Ethelbert was born in East Anglia in the late eighth century. He journeyed to Mercia to seek the hand of Aelfrytha, the daughter of King Offa of Mercia. For political reasons, Offa had the young King Ethelbert murdered (traditionally on 20 May in 794) at Marden, five miles north of Hereford.

To this bare outline must be added more elaborate stories or legends of his life, which have passed down to us through several medieval writers. These weave together traditions associated with Ethelbert's life and death: a spring rose at the site of his beheading; the body was taken by ox-cart to what is now Hereford; on the journey the head fell from the cart; it was rescued by a blind man, who received his sight. Certainly, Ethelbert's body was buried at Hereford Cathedral and became the centre of a thriving pilgrimage cult until the fourteenth century, when it was eclipsed by the newer cult of St Thomas Cantilupe. Little is heard of Ethelbert's relics until after the twelfth century, but it is known that his head was a focus of devotion at Westminster Abbey until the

Shrine of St Ethelbert, Hereford Cathedral (2007)

Dissolution. Representations of Ethelbert may be found in several places in Hereford Cathedral – a defaced fourteenth-century statue is placed near the high altar; there are images of him in several stained-glass windows and there is a nineteenth-century marble representation of Ethelbert's beheading in the pavement in the chancel. In addition, Ethelbert is commemorated on the cathedral seal and by an ancient stone structure near the cathedral, known as 'St Ethelbert's Well'. The cathedral is responsible for the care of two ancient hospitals or groups of almshouses – one of these is St Ethelbert's Hospital in Castle Street. The saint is also remembered at Marden, where he died, and where within the church itself is 'St Ethelbert's Well'. In 2007, a new shrine-like structure was placed in the retro-choir of Hereford Cathedral, on the site generally associated with Ethelbert's original shrine. Designed by Robert Kilgour, it encompasses a central pillar and has on its surfaces 13 icons, by Peter Murphy, telling the story of the saint. The structure is inscribed with words from St Luke's Gospel, linking Ethelbert's own suffering with that of Jesus Christ:

Jesus said: 'All who want to be followers of mine must renounce self. Day after day they must take up their cross and follow me.' (Luke 9.23)

The shrine is used liturgically as a focus for processions on the feast of St Ethelbert and each Friday when prayers are offered for peace and justice in the world.

Notes

1 See pamphlet produced for shrine rededication, 1993.

2 See H. Williams (ed.), 2012, *A Shrine Restored*, Red Dot Publications: Friends of St Davids Cathedral.

3 *Friends of Lichfield Cathedral, 36th annual report*, 1973, pp. 6–7.

4 *Friends of Lichfield Cathedral, 61st annual report*, 1998, p. 6.

5 *Friends of Lichfield Cathedral, 62nd annual report*, 1999, p. 11.

6 Conversations with the dean of Lichfield and administrator of St Chad's, Birmingham, June/July 2013.

7 C. Stubbs, 1898, *Handbook to the Cathedral Church of Ely, Illustrations and Plans*.

8 See photograph in P. Hankey, 1967, *Ely Cathedral*, London: Pitkin.

9 See P. Nixon, 2012, *St Cuthbert of Durham*, Stroud: Amverley, p. 88.

10 See J. Munns, 2015, 'Twentieth century art work', in D. Brown (ed.), *Durham Cathedral – History, Fabric and Culture*, New Haven and London: Yale University Press, pp. 254–5.

11 See Munns, 'Twentieth century art work', pp. 254–5.

12 Preface to *Winchester Cathedral Record*, vol. 31, 1962, pp. 1–2.

13 See C. Wilson, 1977, *The Shrines of St William of York*, Yorkshire Museums.

14 Bishop Sanderson in B. Willis, 1730, *Survey of the Cathedrals of Lincoln, Ely, Oxford and Peterborough*, London, p. 8.

15 J. Crook, 2011, *English Medieval Shrines*, Woodbridge: Boydell Press, pp. 265–6.

16 E. Venables, 1884, *Architectural History of Lincoln Cathedral*, London: James Williamson.

17 *Lincoln Diocesan Magazine (LDM)*, vol. xviii, no. 187, April 1902, p. 54.

18 The 700th anniversary of the death of St Hugh in 1200.

19 *LDM*, December 1902, p. 179.

20 R. E. G. Cole and J. O. Johnston, 1925, *The Body of St Hugh*, p. 25.

21 J. H. Srawley, 1949, *The Story of Lincoln Minster*, London: Raphael Tuck, p. 60.

22 D. Marcombe, 2000, *The Saint and the Swan: The Life and Times of St Hugh of Lincoln*, Lincoln Cathedral Publications, p. 11.

23 Marcombe, *Saint and the Swan*, p. 58.

24 R. Dally, 1831, *The Chichester Guide*, Chichester; P. Binstead and R. Willis, 1861, *The Architectural History of Chichester Cathedral*, Chichester: Mason.

25 M. Hobbs (ed.), *Chichester Cathedral – An Historical Survey*, Chichester: Phillimore, p. 36.

26 A. Duncan-Jones, 1945, *The Chichester Customary*, London: SPCK, pp. 40–1.

27 *Songs of Praise*, 1926, London: Oxford University Press.

28 Sermon preached by Canon Henry Mayr-Harting at Christ Church, Oxford, 3 November 2002.

29 See J. Rayne-David, 2010, *Walsingham – England's National Shrine of Our Lady*, London: St Paul's.

30 See the catalogue of the fragments in W. J. Britnell and K. Watson, 1994, 'Saint Melangell's Shrine, Pennant Melangell', *The Montgomery Collections, Journal of the Powysland Club*, 82, pp. 147–66.

31 G. Marshall, 1930, 'The Shrine of St Thomas de Cantilupe in Hereford Cathedral', in *Transactions of the Woolhope Naturalists' Field Club*, 1930, pp. 34–50.

32 P. Burman and K. Nugents (eds), 1982, *Prophecy and Vision*, Committee for Prophecy and Vision.

33 N. Rathbone, 1982, 'The Radiance of Sanctity', in M. Jancey (ed.), *St Thomas Cantilupe: Essays in his Honour*, Hereford: Friends of Hereford Cathedral, p. 187.

34 R. Shoesmith, Summary Report, and N. Coldstream, 1998, Report 6418/1/10.

8

Postscript – experience at the shrine yesterday and today

While descriptions of shrines of the saints in medieval times are common and often quite detailed, references to what actually happened when pilgrims arrived at the shrines are more rare. The most important sources for pilgrim activities are the accounts of miracles at the shrine or miracula. These are often the pilgrims' own stories and give us a fascinating insight into the mentality and behaviour of ordinary pilgrims. Miracula are generally concerned with details of a malady and its miraculous cure rather than with how a pilgrim gave thanks at the shrine. Other documents – bishops' registers, church accounts and chronicles – add to the picture. From these we can deduce some of the atmosphere and activities that would have occurred.

Shrines were centres of frenetic activity. They were often surrounded by sick people; indeed, there are references to the sick actually being chained to shrines overnight.

Shrines were the climax of the pilgrim experience. Pilgrims frequently entered through the west door of a cathedral and were guided through aisles and screens, each stage increasing the sense of expectation and awe. Often shrines were placed east of the high altar, thus increasing further the sense of the 'holy of holies' in the mind of the pilgrim.

Shrines were not quiet, prayerful places. Pilgrims certainly prayed, but they essentially acted out their prayer. Wax models were bought and left at the shrine – often in the shape of the part of the body prayed for. Candles were bought – often of a length equivalent to the height of the person prayed for.

Niches along the length of the shrine would have been filled with pilgrims kneeling, in some cases making every effort to squeeze their bodies through the apertures to be as near as possible to the relics of the saint.

Shrines were places where offerings were made – sometimes monetary, sometimes gifts of jewels. In many cases, a watching chamber was built nearby, with a guardian watching closely the activities of pilgrims.[1]

Above all, shrines were places where the medieval pilgrim presented their feelings of helplessness and asked the question, 'Why?' Pilgrims brought to the shrine their puzzlement at the harshness of life – cruel disease and sudden death – and sought there not only answers to the insoluble questions of life but also a response in the form of practical action from the saint.

What of today? Can we find any parallels between the effect of shrines in pre-Reformation times and how revived shrines are used today?

The following observations are made from surveys made at three shrines – Durham, Hereford and St Albans – and their results follow surprisingly similar patterns.

Shrines as places of prayer

Most shrines have opportunities for pilgrims to write and leave their prayers. Sometimes special cards are provided and pilgrims are assured that the prayers they write will be used at cathedral worship on a future occasion.

In analysing a cross-section of prayers left at the shrine, researchers at Durham report the following percentages of 'intentions',[2] and examples from other shrines are included to show typical responses.

Prayer to departed relatives (24 per cent)

- I miss you Nicholas Michael, died age 20. Your loving mother – we will meet again.
- Happy Father's Day.
- God bless you Paul – we have never forgotten you. Rest in peace. Love Mum and Dad.

Prayer about departed relatives (18 per cent)

- For Margaret Withers, who died recently of cancer.
- I pray for my grandfather, Thomas, who died thirty years ago today. May he rest in peace – he is always loved and missed.

For a variety of relatives and friends on numerous topics (16 per cent)

- For Mum and Dad – keep them safe in your care in their old age.
- That Jessica will be able to work out her problems around her severe disability and health problems of her two sons.
- A prayer for mothers, wives and children whose men returned from war broken physically or as changed people.
- For Sophie on her third birthday.

Seeking luck or health (12 per cent)

- For help with my examinations.
- For help in my job interview.
- To keep myself family and friends and loved ones free from evil.

Prayer beginning 'Dear God' (11 per cent)

- Dear God, bless Owen in his disappointment – lift his spirits. Amen.
- Dear God remind us whenever our lives get hard, make sure we still think of others.

Prayer for sick people, asking for their health or comfort (9 per cent)

- Claire, my friend, who has been diagnosed with cancer.
- For John, recovering from a stroke.
- Healing, please, for Shirley.

Prayer for blessing or peace for the world or for individuals (5 per cent)

- For the work of 'Save the Children' in Gaza and Syria.
- That all the people of the world learn to live together in peace with each other.
- Happiness and peace for all beings.
- World peace.

Non-English prayers (5 per cent)

Prayers to the saint associated with the shrine (1 per cent)

- St Thomas, stay with Robert and make him well.

In commenting on the nature of these prayers, Douglas Davies writes:

> In terms of a personal word of analysis it seems to be that what stands out above all is the deep relatedness of people. These prayers do not depict isolated selves engaged in a 'self-religion'. Even when, as is often the case, the person is deeply moved, worried or concerned, the matter remains focused on their relationships, family and friends. The only tendency to strong self-reference comes in the 'luck' focused prayers that often ask for success in exams and career. The form most prayers take, whether 'liturgical-like' or completely formal, reveals the spectrum of emotions from raw grief to calm remembrance. Given the strong interpersonal and often intergenerational dimension to these prayers, it is obvious that this pattern of communication through the sheer availability of paper for prayers brings a personal immediacy to the spacious architecture of the cathedral.[3]

Those involved in surveys at St Albans give insights into the reasons for people's visits to the shrine: [4]

> *Why do you light a candle at the shrine here?*
> To offer a prayer.
> To remember departed loved ones.
> For special people.
> To show respect.
> As a pilgrim.
> For my inner calm.
> Thanksgiving.
> To remember God.

Those who assisted in the survey at Hereford noted the great variety of places from which visitors came. On just one day, there were pilgrims from the USA, Scotland, Holland, Winchester, Portsmouth, Swansea, Kidderminster, Leicester and Hereford.

One thing is certain – those who leave prayers at the shrines are from a huge variety of backgrounds. It is possible that only a small percentage have any particular religious persuasion and even fewer seem to make their prayers to the saint commemorated, and yet somehow the atmosphere of the place draws them and pilgrims often report on how their visit has taught them a little more about the shrine's own saints. Few, if any, see the shrine as inappropriate in an Anglican place of worship, although one prayer written at the Hereford shrine states: 'Whatever happened to the Reformation?'

In many ways, pilgrims are drawn to the shrine for the same reasons as their medieval forebears. People today, as then, are faced with questions for which there seem to be no answers – pain, illness, disappointment, death. Now, as then, when there is no easy answer, pilgrims feel moved to 'do' something – to light a candle, to write a prayer. Now, as then, the saint commemorated seems to provide some degree of help and encouragement and comfort. Some have suggested that what pilgrims do at the shrines today is very similar to the behaviour at roadside shrines: an inexplicable happening has no answers but somehow demands a human response – flowers, messages, toys. Some writers have pointed to an increase in this kind of response since the outpouring of grief associated with the death of Princess Diana in 1997 – the so-called 'Diana effect'.

In summary, a question and answer, as published in *Church Times*:

Q. In several English cathedrals, there used to be a shrine of a saint, containing a relic. Some have been rebuilt, copied or left as a space for prayer ... In each destroyed shrine, there remains material, even if only the flooring, that once touched the relics. Can this be justifiably regarded as a secondary relic? May we regard a reconstruction or replica as a true shrine and hope for miracles?

A. Hereford Cathedral is one of a handful of English cathedrals where substantial parts of the saint's shrine have survived, and, in recent years, these remains have, in several cases, been restored and developed. I can think of only two major shrines where the saint's body remains – Westminster Abbey and Durham Cathedral – but others, such as Hereford, St Albans and Chichester, do possess small relics that have been returned to their original resting place.

In 'restoring' medieval shrines, we are not, I think, aiming to recreate a 'pre-Reformation cult'. It is true that these shrines were powerful focuses of prayer and healing: in Hereford alone, at the shrine of St Thomas of Hereford between 1287 and 1307 some 470 miracles are recorded (second only to Canterbury's Thomas, where more than 600 are recorded). Many of the healing miracles were dramatic and immediate. But today, restored shrines are there, I think, to provide a focus for prayer, intercession and healing in the broadest sense. We have certainly not restored them with the intention of 'hoping for miracles'.

While some may regard such an interpretation of medieval practice as rather un-Anglican, there is little doubt that these shrines are places where the boundaries between heaven and earth are extremely thin.

Visitors and pilgrims feel this powerfully, and our shrine's intercession board is nearly always full of the most moving prayers – and, yes, the same people might well testify to healing that they have experienced at these places.[5]

Candles lit at the shrine of St Thomas of Hereford

Notes

1 See B. Nilson, 1999, 'The Medieval Experience at the Shrine', in J. Stopford, *Pilgrimage Explored*, York: York Medieval Press, pp. 95–122.

2 D. D. Davies, 2013, *Popular Prayers Written at Durham Cathedral: Contemporary Cameos*, Centre for Death and Life Studies, Department of Theology and Religion, Durham University.

3 Davies, *Popular Prayers*, p. 17.

4 Interviews conducted at St Albans, August 2014.

5 *Church Times*, 22 October 2010.

Bibliography

Anson, P. F., 1960, *Fashions in Church Furnishings*, London: Faith Press.

Archbishops' Council, 2004, *Mission-Shaped Church: Church Planting and Fresh Expressions of Church in a Changing Context*, London: Church House Publishing.

Atterbury, P. and Wainwright, C. (eds), 1994, *Pugin: A Gothic Passion*, New-haven and London: Yale University Press.

Aylmer, G. E. and Cant, R. (eds), 1977, *A History of York Minster*, Oxford: Clarendon Press.

Aylmer, G. E. and Tiller, J. (eds), 2000, *Hereford Cathedral – A History*, London: Hambledon.

Baring-Gould, S., 1872, *Lives of the Saints*, 2nd edn, London: John Hodges.

Barrett, P., 1993, *Barchester: English Cathedral Life in the Nineteenth Century*, London: SPCK.

Bartholomew, C. and Hughes, F. (eds), 2004, *Explorations in a Christian Theology of Pilgrimage*, Aldershot: Ashgate.

Bennett, F., 1925, *The Nature of a Cathedral*, Chester: Philipson & Golder.

Bentley, J., 1985, *Restless Bones: The Story of Relics*, London: Constable.

Bethell, D., 1972, 'The making of a twelfth-century relic collection', in G. J. Cumming and D. Baker (eds), *Popular Belief and Practice*, Cambridge: Cambridge University Press.

Brierley, P., 1991, *Christian England*, London: Marc Europe.

Brown, C., 2001, *The Death of Christian Britain*, London: Routledge.

Bruce, S., 2002, *God is Dead: Secularisation in the West*, Oxford: Blackwell.

Bussby, F., 1979, *Winchester Cathedral 1079–1979*, Southampton: Paul Cave Publications.

Butler, J. R., 1996, *The Quest for Becket's Bones: The Mystery of the Relics of St Thomas of Canterbury*, New Haven, CT and London: Yale University Press.

Carmichael, D., Hubert, J. and Reeve, B., 1994, *Sacred Sites, Sacred Places*, London: Routledge.

Carpenter, E., 1966, *House of Kings*, London: John Baker.

Cobb, G., 1980, *English Cathedrals: The Forgotten Centuries*, London: Thames and Hudson.

Caviness, M. H., 1977, *The Early Stained Glass of Canterbury Cathedral, c.1175–1220*, Princeton, NJ: Medieval Academy of America.

Chadwick, O., 1990, *The Spirit of the Oxford Movement*, Cambridge: Cambridge University Press.

Chadwick, O., 1966, *The Victorian Church*, London: Adam and Charles Black.

Chandler, M., 2003, *An Introduction to the Oxford Movement*, London: SPCK.

Colgrave, B. and Mynors, R. (eds), 1992, *Bede, Ecclesiastical History of the English People*, Oxford: Oxford University Press.

Collinson, P., Ramsey, N. and Sparks, M. (eds), 1995, *A History of Canterbury Cathedral*, Oxford: Oxford University Press.

Crook, J., 2011, *English Medieval Shrines*, Woodbridge: Boydell Press.

Davie, G., 1994, *Religion in Britain since 1945*, Oxford: Blackwell.

Davies, J. G., 1988, *Pilgrimage Yesterday and Today – Why? Where? How?* London: SCM Press.

Dickens, A. D., 1974, The *English Reformation*, London: Fontana.

Dickenson, J. C., 1956, *The Shrine of Our Lady of Walsingham*, Cambridge: Cambridge University Press.

Duffy, E., 1992, 2nd edn 2005, *The Stripping of the Altars: Traditional Religion in England 1400–1580*, New Haven, CT and London: Yale University Press.

Duncan-Jones, A., 1945, *The Chichester Customary*, London: SPCK.

Fincham, K. and Tyacke, N., 2007, *Altars Restored: The Changing Face of English Religious Worship, 1547–c.1700*, London: Oxford University Press.

Finucane, R., 1977/95, *Miracles and Pilgrims: Popular Beliefs in Medieval England*, London: Macmillan.

Goodhew, D. (ed.), 2011, *Church Growth in Britain, 1980 to the Present*, Aldershot: Ashgate, 2011.

Greenslade, M. W., 1996, *Saint Chad of Lichfield and Birmingham*, Archdiocese of Birmingham Historical Commission.

Haigh, C. (ed.), 1987, *The English Reformation Revised*, Cambridge: Cambridge University Press.

Heelas, P. and Woodhead, L., 2005, *The Spiritual Revolution: Why Religion is Giving Way to Spirituality*, Oxford: Blackwell.

Herbert, A., Martin, P. and Thomas, G. (eds), 2008, *St Albans, Cathedral and Abbey*, Fraternity of the Friends of St Albans Abbey.

Hobbs, M. (ed.), 1994, *Chichester Cathedral: An Historical Survey*, Chichester: Phillimore.

Inge, J., 2003, *A Christian Theology of Place*, Aldershot: Ashgate.

Jancey, M. (ed.), 1982, *St Thomas Cantilupe: Essays in his Honour*, Hereford: Friends of Hereford Cathedral.

Lehmberg, S. E., 1996, *Cathedrals Under Siege: Cathedrals in English Society 1600–1700*, Exeter: Exeter University Press.

MacKenzie, I. M. (ed.), 1996, *Cathedrals Now: Their Use and Place in Society*, Norwich, Canterbury Press.

Mayhew Smith, N., 2010, *Britain's Holiest Places*, Bristol: Lifestyle Press.

Nilson, B., 1998, *Cathedral Shrines of England*, Woodbridge: Boydell Press.

Norman, E., 1985, *Roman Catholicism in England from the Elizabethan Settlement to the Second Vatican Council*, Oxford: Oxford University Press.

Meadows, P. and Ramsay, N., 2003, *A History of Ely Cathedral*, Woodbridge: Boydell Press.

Owen, D. (ed.), 1994, *A History of Lincoln Minster*, Cambridge: Cambridge University Press.

Nockles, P., 1994, *The Oxford Movement in Context 1760–1850*, Cambridge: Cambridge University Press, 1994.

Perham, M., 1979, *The Communion of Saints*, London: Alcuin Club/SPCK.

Platten, S. and Lewis C. (eds), 1998, *Flagships of the Spirit: Cathedrals in Society*, London: Darton, Longman and Todd.

Platten, S. and Lewis C. (eds), 2006, *Dreaming Spires: Cathedrals in a New Age*, London: SPCK.

Shackley, M., 2001, *Managing Sacred Sites: Service Provision and Visitors' Experience*, London: Thomson.

Stopford, J., 1999, *Pilgrimage Explored*, York: York Medieval Press.

Sumption, J., 1975, *Pilgrimage: An Image of Medieval Religion*, Totowa, NJ: Rowman & Littlefield.

Symondson, A. and Bucknell, S., 2006, *Sir Ninian Comper: An Introduction to His Life and Work, with Complete Gazeteer*, London: Spire Books.

Trowles, T., 2005, *A Bibliography of Westminster Abbey*, Woodbridge: Boydell Press.

Welander, D., 1991, *The History, Art and Architecture of Gloucester Cathedral*, Stroud: Alan Sutton.

Wilson, C., 1997, *The Atlas of Holy Places and Sacred Sites*, New York: Reed Publishing.

Woodhead, L. and Catto, R., 2012, *Religious Change in Modern Britain*, London: Routledge.

Wyn Evans, J. and Wooding, J. M. (eds), 2007, *St David of Wales: Cult, Church and Nation*, Woodbridge: Boydell Press.

Yates, N., 2008, *Liturgical Space: Christian Worship and Church Buildings in Western Europe, 1500–2000*, Aldershot: Ashgate.

Yelton, M., 2006, *Alfred Hope Patten and the Shrine of Our Lady of Walsingham*, Norwich: Canterbury Press.

Index